A JOHN CATT PUBLICATION

T0273474

LET'S TALK ABOUT FLEX

Flipping the flexible working narrative for education

EMMA TURNER

First published 2020

by John Catt Educational Ltd,
15 Riduna Park, Station Road,
Melton, Woodbridge IP12 1QT

Tel: +44 (0) 1394 389850
Fax: +44 (0) 1394 386893
Email: enquiries@johncatt.com
Website: www.johncatt.com

© **2020 Emma Turner**

All rights reserved.

No part of this publication may be reproduced, stored
in a retrieval system, transmitted in any form or by
any means, electronic, mechanical, photocopying,
recording, or otherwise, without the prior permission
of the publishers.

Opinions expressed in this publication are those
of the contributors and are not necessarily those
of the publishers or the editors. We cannot accept
responsibility for any errors or omissions.

ISBN: 978 1 913622 31 2

Set and designed by John Catt Educational Limited

To Mitcho and memories

Praise for Let's Talk About Flex

I love the energy, humour and optimism of this book. A must-read for all who believe in liberating school leadership – this offers a practical, career-affirming approach and is an absolute delight to read.

Dame Alison Peacock, Chief Executive of the Chartered College of Teaching

This is a groundbreaking book and an exceptionally good read. Emma has a gift for a musical metaphor, stretched to provide remarkable insights into the possibilities and many of the barriers to flexible working. If any other sector was haemorrhaging highly trained and capable staff with such rapidity, then there would be serious questions asked. Emma poses these questions and provides a range of sensible solutions. We need to stop paying lip service to teacher retention, start taking it seriously and this book points to the way to take solid steps to get there.

Mary Myatt, education adviser, speaker and author

As always, Emma's delightfully accessible and humorous style combines with important substance and powerful messages. This book raises issues that need to be taken seriously by the teaching profession but also offers solutions. It's a must-read both for school leaders and for those who want to find ways of making flexible working a personal way forward.'

Professor Samantha Twiselton OBE, Director of Sheffield Institute of Education and Vice President (external) of Chartered College of Teaching

Emma Turner has a gift for communicating serious ideas in the most human and engaging of ways. She explores all the details, for employers and flexible workers – the give and take, the realities and possibilities, the money, the time – all whilst dancing joyously to her kitchen disco. If you know Emma, this is partly metaphorical and partly literal. And that's the joy of this book! Flexible working allows people to have fulfilling productive working lives and healthy home lives with arrangements that flex and change as they need to. It's still not as normalised as it should be but, with Emma's guidance, hopefully more people will see just how well it can be done.

Tom Sherrington, author, speaker and former headteacher

This book is a Bohemian Rhapsody. Just like Queen's iconic anthem, Emma mixes the right amount of crazy, with artistry, humour and genius to passionately explain a hugely important and often misunderstood concept. It is life-changing and brilliant. If it was a poster, it would be taking pride of place right next to Freddie.

Richard Gerver, author, speaker and former headteacher

As one of the most successful change-makers in education, Emma has written another game-changer for the staffroom – both on and offline. This will be top of our GEC list for educational providers from early years to post 16 as it is a practical and dynamic way to get #SmashingStereotypes. Emma not only talks in a language you can understand but also has actual lived experience as a working professional who has been a trailblazer for everything flexible working. This book enables you to hear all the tips and tricks that helped her make such a success of both her career and continue being a present parent, invites you to reflect on how this will work for you with some giggles along the way. I suggest you buy this book, devour it immediately and then march into your setting and demand flexible working for your entire staffroom.

Nic Ponsford, co-CEO and Founder of the GEC (FRSA)

Let's Talk About Flex encourages us to think differently about historical Infrastructure and working practices so that we can capitalise on the extraordinary potential of flexible ways of working. Emma unpicks the demographics of teachers aged 31-39 so it now seems ridiculous that school leaders don't do all they can to retain these amazing teachers, the majority of whom are still women. We are given excellent advice on how to develop more flex to the benefit of all and the strength of this book is the importance given to the need for diverse approaches and thinking.

Vivienne Porritt, education and leadership consultant, national leader of WomenEd

With a combination of optimism and rigorous argument, Emma breaks down the superficial protests we've been hearing for years against flexible working and provides a systematic, passionate and compelling argument for flexible working.

Dr Emma Kell, author, speaker and teacher

Her grit and determination to trail blaze and make flex working work shines through every chapter.

Alison Kriel, education consultant and CEO of Amaya Trust

This is a very timely book from Emma Turner and one I strongly suspect will become a reference book for all things with regards to flexible working.

Bukky Yusuf, teacher, consultant and qualified coach

I love Emma Turner's writing: I find it joyful and refreshing, characterised by energy, enthusiasm, honesty and humour.

Jill Berry, leadership consultant, former headteacher and author

This is an equally powerful read for those considering making a flexible request as it is for those on the other side of the desk – It's a musical manifesto for flexible working in education.

Helena Marsh, Principal at Linton Village College

Not only does it burst the doors off preconceived ideas around flexible working which are shown to be limited, blinkered and embarrassingly outdated at times, it takes leaders and educators by the hand and gently shows them how it could work.

Clementine Stewart, Senior Head of Prep at Surbiton High School

Let's Talk About Flex welcomes you on to the dancefloor but emphasises that everyone is invited, this party is not just for the mothers in our schools. Yet, again, she has me laughing out loud whilst simultaneously thinking very hard!

Hannah Wilson, headteacher and independent consultant

Emma Turner knows her stuff on policy and process when it comes to all matter of flexible working – bringing knowledge and lived experience to the topic that could revolutionise the profession as a whole.

Kat Howard, author, assistant principal and Founder of Litdrive UK

Emma's wisdom and practical advice challenges the way we approach our work and will prove motivational and transformational.

Jamie Thom, author, teacher and podcast host

This is must-read for anyone considering how to promote flexible working for themselves or their organisation.

Lucy Flower, regional representative for WomenEd and MTPT, TES columnist and music teacher

Acknowledgements

There are so many people in my 'flexible friends' crew who I must extend warm thanks, big smiles and a little Turner happy dance to. As you read this book, you will realise the true flexi champions are my parents and immediate family, instilling in me the confidence to always ask the question has simply been the greatest gift. Thanks must also go to my wonderful buddy Claire Moran (Mitcho) who, as we set up the co-headship back in 2009, was my fabulous flexi adventuring buddy and our escapades and learning during those early flexi leadership years alongside her unwavering friendship, continue to inspire me.

To the WomenEd community who have given me opportunities to share my story, as well as advice and guidance when I have had a wobble, and helped me to continue to challenge systems at every level, I'm sending you the biggest virtual hug. Vivienne, Hannah, Alison K., Jill, Alison P., Sam, Debs, Jules, Liz, Keziah, Bukky and so many more within the community. We are stronger together and thank you so much for all that you do. To Jonny and Stricko, for agreeing to write the foreword. Your voices and support give this argument exactly what it needs, a huge kick into the forefront of leaders' minds. Thank you so much for championing the cause and for allowing me to pick your brains and annoy the hell out of you both with chat about biscuits, Frazzles and Vimto.

Thanks to all of team secondary who have helped to shape a lot of the framing around post Key Stage 2 flex. To Kat and Nimish, I wouldn't have had the confidence to write this without your words of wisdom and experience. Thanks especially to Kat for inviting me to debut my talk on flex at her own book launch back in February. This book is technically your fault! Thanks for always being the voice of reason and clarity. You have no idea how much I value your support, friendship and input.

I cannot fail to thank the wonderful Richard Gerver and Rod Berger for always believing in me. Thank you for opening so many doors and for championing this little Leicester lass. You have both created so many opportunities for me and I'm so grateful. Nic and the crew at GEC also deserve a huge thank you for the amazing work they're doing within the area of flex. Thanks for having me as an ambassador – still haven't received the ambassadorial Ferrero Rocher yet though! A big thanks too to my employers at Discovery, James and Paul. They put up with all my hare-brained ideas, give me the freedom and opportunity to shape my own career and are always my biggest edu-champions and greatest cheerleaders. Thank you so much for believing in me – here's to our next adventures.

Finally, to my little trinity of chaos at home, thank you for being the reason I do everything I do. May you forever be brave, kind and – just like nanny and granddad – always ask the question for yourself and on behalf of others who may not be able to, because 'if you don't ask, you don't get'.

Contents

Foreword

By Sam Strickland and Jonny Uttley

As the lyrics to the well-known dance track 'Insomnia' by Faithless say: 'I can't get no sleep'. How often as a teacher have you felt that sleep is a luxury? If you can just squeeze in another hour of work, mark a few more books, plan another lesson, respond to a few more emails, then your day tomorrow will be just that little bit easier. Over time, however, you begin to burn the candle at both ends, becoming jaded, ill and, at the very worst, burnt out. This in turn causes people to leave the profession despite having shown so much potential and promise as a trainee teacher. Worse still, people from afar see what is going on in our profession and think to themselves 'thanks but no thanks'. The notion that teachers work from 9am to 3pm and have 13 weeks off a year is a fallacy.

I would like to iron out a fact; teaching is not an easy profession. It never has been and it probably never will be. I liken teaching to having to serve as a stand-up comic for five or six hours a day, five days a week, plus all of the extra work that has to be done in your own time. The key difference though is that no one would expect a stand-up to go on tour and perform a five to six-hour set daily. I have seen people describe some teachers as martyrs or that they should be able to regulate their own workload. To some extent this may be true. However, I do see it as the responsibility of senior leaders, especially the head, in their 'magic ivory tower' to do something to rationalise staff workload and support their lifestyle.

I have heard countless times that 'teaching should hurt,' or that 'if you are not burnt out by the end of a term then you have not been doing it right'. For some, teaching can be a highway to hell, leading us to an express stairway to heaven. A lot has been written about reducing teacher workload, with strategies ranging from email embargos and increased faculty time, to rationalising data drops and approaches to marking, to supporting staff with the centralisation of behaviour. In some schools there are notable and enviable workload charters, which are actually living and breathing pledges to support staff workload. All of this is great but if we truly want to enter a happy boogie wonderland then more still can be done.

This is where Emma leads the charge. Her disco-tech jukebox of key chapters will take you on a journey into the world of flexible working. She outlines succinctly the Department of Education's lofty ambition for allowing flexible working to take place in schools but then eloquently builds on this with her own extensive experience. Every chapter is packed with extensive examples of how people can be supported with managing their job and their own life. The days where flexible working was something to be frowned upon, seen as an inconvenience or that the member of staff in question making 'that request' really is lazy, lazy, lazy should be a thing of the past. The reasons people want to work flexibly are many and varied. The trick that is often missed is that if you treat staff well not only will they be happier in their job, not only will they stick around and work for you for longer but they will actually be more – not less – productive.

Enjoy the read, it will make you think, it will make you want to make you challenge the status quo and it will make you consider that the dinosaur age really does need to become extinct. Teaching should not hurt, quite the reverse.

Sam Strickland, Principal of Duston School in Northamptonshire and author of Education Exposed and Education Exposed 2

✶✶

Contributing a foreword to this book is both very straightforward and really difficult. Straightforward in that there are so many great things to talk about in this book; difficult as I do not have Emma's genius for incorporating music. But I'll give it a go!

There is an overwhelming amount of research that shows the biggest impact we can have on outcomes for young people and the success of schools is to put the best teachers we can in front of classes. I know, I know, as Tony Hadley says it's 'Obvious'. Yet despite its obviousness, too many schools undermine it by failing to think flexibly in the broadest sense. An outdated perception of how school staff should work means that too many great teachers have been lost to schools and to the young people in them when all that is needed is some thought about how to remove any barriers to keeping great teachers and leaders.

It's only taken a global pandemic to get the education system to wake up to what flexible working might mean! Back in March we were all sent home and told to lead schools and teach children but to do it without coming onto the school site. We discovered Microsoft Teams and Zoom. Some suddenly found out that presenteeism wasn't the be-all-and-end-all and that being in school from 8am to 5pm five days a week is not actually an essential criterion for being a brilliant teacher or leader. Looking back on the way things were in many schools, I'm pretty sure Frank and Nancy would call it 'Somethin' Stupid'.

So, if the penny is dropping that children need us to keep our great teachers and leaders and the last few months have shown us there are lots of different ways of working, what should we do next? Just do like Beyonce and 'Listen'. Listen to Emma Turner and the people like Emma up and down the country. People who get what flexible working really means, those who live it every day, those who understand it all – the complexities and the opportunities. Most importantly, listen to the people whose track records show beyond a shadow of a doubt that schools that develop real cultures of flexibility can become some of the best schools to work in and, subsequently, some of the best schools for children to attend.

This book is so packed full of wisdom, experience and common-sense thinking, written by someone with enormous credibility and gentle wit – a combination that is so persuasive it takes us into the realm of the no-brainer. As with any good kitchen disco, we can refuse to take part or just go for it. And so with thinking about flexible working we can refuse to engage or seize the chance. Which finally brings me to my guilty secret – I'm a fan of country music! As you start to read this brilliant book, think about what Lee Ann Womack says about when we face a choice between sitting it out and dancing: 'I Hope You Dance'.

Jonny Uttley, CEO of The Education Alliance Multi-Academy Trust and author of Putting Staff First

Introduction: The kitchen disco

If you know me, you know I love a disco and a dance. Our kitchen every day is my dancefloor and my three kids and I are often found having a 'kitchen disco' during breakfast as we belt out the lyrics and bust a few enthusiastic – but all too often uncoordinated – moves over the cereal or the toast. Nothing starts the day like a dance around to something loud, lively and uplifting. Our taste is eclectic, often cheesy and varied but one thing unites it all and that is that we leave smiling.

Now if you've just read the above and think that I'm writing about flexible working because I have three small children and, therefore, work part-time and that's what flexible working constitutes then you'd be a little bit right but also a great big dollop of wrong. I've worked flexibly in education since 2004 in a mixture of full-time and part-time roles, in teacher and leadership and co-headship roles for national strategies, for local authorities and for a MAT. I've worked for myself, I've worked for an employer and sometimes I've done both. Because the narrative around flexible working needs flipping. Many people think they know what flexible working is but when questioned, it becomes clear that their view is often very narrow and more often than not falls into the above unbelievably narrow and frustrating stereotype of 'mum with a young family working part-time'. It's the default vision of flexible working for so many people and why the whole conversation needs to open up. It's like saying 'music' and thinking that this only encompasses pop or classical rather than a myriad of genres and performers. There's then the whole

Covid-19 lockdown thing which I'll write about in detail later, but from the outset let's just get one thing straight: the working practices which went on in lockdown were not flexible working. Yes, they shone a light on a lot of opportunities and challenges for flexible working, but they were categorically not flexible working. To stick with the musical theme, real flexible working practices are beautiful orchestral masterpieces involving an entire ensemble all playing in time and in tune to create something well practised, rehearsed and inspirational. What we had in the pandemic lockdown was the musical equivalent initially of an unsupervised toddler with a tambourine and at the very best a self-taught squeaking recorder playing by a seven-year-old. That is not to say our toddler tambourine player and seven-year-old squeaker won't grow into something tuneful and beautiful but we must not kid ourselves that our knee jerk responses to home working practices amid a global pandemic were flexible working masterpieces.

It's not just the breakfast table which is party to my love of a dance. I often use music in my training and CPD sessions and it's become somewhat of a given that I cannot facilitate, deliver, write or present without some sort of accompanying soundtrack. Music to me is what makes me happy, makes me brave, makes me believe, gives me comfort and stirs so many memories. Whenever I want to remember anything I end up making it into a song of some sort and I have this awful habit of linking anything anyone says to a song lyric. Former colleagues know all too well that I am prone to busting out anything from Beyoncé (complete with dance routine) on a wheeled office chair to entire Run-DMC songs and complete '90s indie back catalogues. It was a running joke at my last school that the Year 6s would come and sing me a song at playtime and I'd end up joining in with them. You've not lived until you've seen my Taylor Swift performed in court shoes and a navy blue suit alongside a group of 11-year-old wannabe popstars.

Anything important to me seems to be tied up in music and my car or my kitchen is my audience-less stage. Believe me though, I'm no singer; I couldn't carry a tune in a bucket but music and its lyrics are what often inspires me to think differently and which have helped to shape much of my thinking around the issues involved in flexible working. With this in mind, each of the lessons I have learnt about flexible working I have linked to the song which matches most. All of these are often on the playlist in my car or on my headphones on the way to an event about flexible working. Be warned though, the songs are not necessarily a representation of my *actual* musical taste and I'd hate for anyone to judge my musical choices based on this list alone as there is more than a fair helping of 'cheese'. However, if you want to find out more about the issues around flexible working and you want to begin to think differently about how we can approach flexible working then this playlist is the perfect starting point.

Grab yourself a wooden spoon microphone, get on that kitchen disco dancefloor and let's talk about *flex*.

Track one: Let's Talk About 'Flex'
Salt-N-Pepa

I get asked to speak about flexible working a lot.

Sometimes it is in and around the subject of the co-headship I was part of back in 2009 for eight years with my wonderful former colleague Claire Moran (nee Mitchell) where we set up one of the first all-female co-headships. Sometimes it is with my parent hat on to talk about balancing family and work life. Other times it is to talk about misconceptions around flexible working and what exactly it is. Whenever anyone has asked me before to 'talk about flex' at an event, I have always ended up humming the song by Salt-N-Pepa with its very similar but slightly more risqué title. It became so much of a running joke that in direct messages on Twitter with some of my edu-colleagues I have even rapped the full song (albeit with slightly altered lyrics) to fit the 'flex' narrative. Don't worry, I can assure you though that the world of hip hop is not due to have another superstar smash onto the scene. My rapping talents leave much to be desired and I think education will remain my spiritual home despite my spirited and very enthusiastic attempts at rap.

Nonetheless, listening to the song and reading an interview from Rolling Stone magazine in 1994 with Salt-N-Pepa made me realise that there is much more in common than just a rhyme between the song title and concept of working flexibly. The lyrics, *Let's tell it how it is, and how it could be; How it was, and of course, how it should be'* are what run through my head before any speaking engagement I have or piece I write around flexible working because flexible working continues to remain somewhat of a taboo or neglected subject. In the same interview, they say, 'It was us being really, really bold and challenging the status quo of radio' and, 'The song was about communication and talking about a subject that nobody wants to talk about. So just from the gate, for me, it was brilliant. Because I knew it would catch everybody's ear, how could it not?'

Now, as a suburban mum of three from the Midlands, I couldn't be further from the world of hip hop but those words on communication and challenging the status quo are what I feel I do every time I am asked to speak about flexible working. It's still in its relative infancy in education and there are still so many barriers, prejudices, assumptions and, occasionally, downright ignorance and fear around the topic that the narrative around it does need a fierce and whole scale shake-up. As another of Salt-N-Pepa's hit single's title states, we need to take the discussion around flexible working and 'push it'.

At the end of each chapter, there will be a series of questions for both those who are employing flexible workers and those who are seeking flexible working opportunities or currently working flexibly. This is not a perfect delineation as obviously some employers work flexibly too but to begin discussions, the following two headings have been used.

Questions to consider

Employers	Flexible workers
Can you name the five main types of flexible working?	Can you name the five main types of flexible working?
How many flexible workers do you have in your organisation?	Do you know if there are other flexible workers in your organisation?
What kinds of roles or levels of responsibility do these flexible workers represent?	What is the range of roles within your organisation which are represented by flexible workers?
What do you feel are the biggest benefits of flexible working?	What would be the benefits of flexible working for you?
What do you feel are the biggest barriers to flexible working?	What would be the biggest barriers and/or downsides to flexible working?
Do you have a flexible working strategy, approach or best practice guide?	Do you know what the procedure is in your organisation for applying for flexible working?

Track two: Waterloo

Abba

Who doesn't love a bit of Abba? You can't fail to be uplifted by at least one of their songs and, in terms of doing things differently and flipping narratives, they were trailblazers during Eurovision 1974 with 'Waterloo', becoming the first winning entry in a language other than that of their home country. Up until 1973, all Eurovision singers had been required to sing in the language of their country but there was a brief lifting of the ban on this between 1973 and 1976 which meant that they were able to sing 'Waterloo' in English. At Eurovision's 50th anniversary celebrations, Waterloo was voted the best winning song of all time, which just goes to show what great things can happen when you lift the bans, challenge the status quo and do things a little differently.

Coincidentally I was born during that ban lifting period and – much like Abba at the time – have always decided to do things just that little bit differently. Perhaps it was something in the mid-70s water! It frustrates me beyond measure when, like their lyrics say, history is always repeating itself. If things never change then there is never progress, there is never learning, there is never the opportunity for development, adventure, success or the possibility of discovering untapped potential. The adage of 'do what you've always done, get what you've always got' seems to morph around flexible working to 'we *must* do what we've always done and preserve exactly what we've got'. The nonsense of this 'if it ain't broke, don't fix it' mentality seems to ignore, like an ostrich with its head in the sand, that in education we are facing an employment crisis. I'm not going to call it a recruitment crisis or, indeed, a retention crisis as we have a lot of qualified teachers in this country. They're just choosing not to work in our schools.

We attract a lot of new teachers every year. We do, however, lose a huge proportion of them within the first few years. If any other company or sector was haemorrhaging highly trained and capable staff with such rapidity, then there would be serious questions asked. Of course, it is a crying shame when we lose a teacher at any stage but to lose an experienced teacher and established team member is much more than a financial and recruitment headache. We cannot see teachers, especially experienced teachers, as expendable because they don't fit a neat historical working pattern. We cannot expect to replace them with cheaper inexperienced staff who temporarily might balance a budget but who deserve to be well supported and developed by experienced and knowledgeable colleagues and mentors, rather than having to find their way in an ever-dwindling pool of experienced practitioners.

I know I developed rapidly as an early career teacher as I was surrounded by brilliant, experienced, wise and wonderful colleagues. Kay, the warm and calm voice of experience as my NQT mentor, a Key Stage 1 veteran whose kind words of reassurance and demonstration of her expertise helped to shape my practice. Gill, the unbelievably knowledgeable and talented deputy of whom I was in total awe and who took the time to talk to me, guide me through what constituted exceptional practice and introduced me to the world of academic research. Mick and Gilly, the exceptional colleagues in my second school whose sheer natural talent, creativity, humour and love of the job and the children showed me daily why education was the greatest vocation in the world. Without colleagues like Kay, Gill, Mick and Gilly I certainly wouldn't have become the teacher I am today or have progressed as quickly with the confidence and knowledge with which they equipped me. We simply cannot insist that in a public service, which serves a modern society, that we fixate rigidly on upholding historical working practices and infrastructures which all too often mean our brightest, our best, our most likely to blossom are driven out and unable to fulfil their potential. The irony is that as teachers we have it drilled into us from day one of our journey as educators that we must meet the needs of all learners for them to fulfil their potential. What a waste it is then to not apply these same principles to the working and professional learning lives of our talented and dedicated educators.

Flexible working might just be the answer. It's not a silver bullet; nothing is ever a complete panacea. However, rather than acting like the violinists on the Titanic who continued to play despite the ship sinking, we need to bang a different drum and the recruitment DJs need to play a different and much more popular tune now we can see that the teaching dancefloor is emptying.

The biggest demographic after retirees to leave teaching are women between the ages of 31 and 40 years old. Let's just unpick this for a moment and not just blithely assume that this is the demographic which might well be leaving for parenthood. Let's look at this from a different point of view. Let's see the demographic as a group of teachers who have completed their initial teacher education and entered the profession at approximately 23. At the very least that's a teacher leaving who has eight years' of experience and at the upper end, 17 years of experience. That is huge. These are not just a group of teachers leaving. These are the mentors, the tutors, the voices of experience and wisdom, the experts, the unconsciously competent professionals who can deal reliably with an unruly class on a wet Friday afternoon, a demanding parent or a serious child protection issue. These are the colleagues who can provide models of excellence, words of comfort and reassurance, they are the keepers of knowledge on the development of the profession and the familiar face for staff and the community. They are the bonds of trust built up over time for students, families, communities and staff. They are the ones who can do an assembly at the drop of a hat, know your data systems, are adept at taking on new ideas because their skills are honed and well developed; their lessons are tried, tested, evaluated and refined. They know what works, what doesn't work, who's who and what's what and we just let them walk out of the door.

Many walk because so many of them believe the job to be undoable alongside their life commitments or believe the doors to roles which provide challenge, growth and development are not open to them. Now how does it feel to know that it is this group who are leaving in droves? There may be one or two leaving in each school but across the country, these lone voices form a massed choir of dissatisfaction. A chorus of disbelief that the profession for which they trained so hard cannot accommodate anything other than a single structural working pattern and, in leadership, sadly this attitude is even more ingrained. We simply cannot let this demographic, alongside our bright new entrants to the profession, be the ones who leave. We need to stem the flow of bodies to the exit doors and instead fling on an absolute floor filler.

It's time to whack on the pioneering edu-Abba.

Questions to consider

Employers	Flexible workers
How many employees left your organisation during the last academic year?	What would be your ideal working pattern?
How many left for promotion/relocation or a move to a similar role?	How many years of experience do you currently have?
How many left due to workload demands?	Do you have regular career development discussions with a coach, mentor or line manager?
Do you currently do exit interviews? Do they discuss flexible working options?	What are your career goals?
Do you regularly review how many of your staff would be interested in flexible working opportunities?	Are you aware of the full range of roles open to you both within and beyond your organisation?
What is the ratio of experienced to early career teachers in your organisation?	Have you experience of mentoring or coaching others?
What is the average time an employee remains in your organisation?	What are your current strengths and areas for development? How will you address these?

Track three: If I Can Dream

Elvis Presley

Goodness me I love a bit of Elvis. If you ever want to belt out a song then you can't go wrong with whacking on a bit of the King, complete with curled lip and iconic stance. When asked to picture Elvis, so many of us will automatically think of either the young fresh-faced Elvis or the bespangled white jumpsuit-wearing 'Vegas' Elvis. However, few of us will picture any of the other versions of the artist whose career spanned both music and film (he actually acted in 33 films). Many of us, despite his amazing success, will have a single default vision of his appearance. We might also recollect his untimely and sad demise, which is often more well-known than some of his artistic achievements. It is having this default vision, such as when we think of Elvis, that all too many people apply when considering the picture of what constitutes flexible working – this can then prevent us from seeing the bigger flexible picture. So, what exactly is flexible working? If it is to be the next huge educational superstar then what exactly are their greatest hits?

Well, let's start by thinking about what flexible working conjures up for you? Think about who might want to work flexibly? How might that flexible working then be modelled? Which roles in organisations are most suited to flexible working? How many flexible workers can an organisation accommodate? All of these are frequently asked questions but also, at the same time, are limiting micro judgements. Just as we leap to our default vision of Elvis, so too do many of us automatically have a stereotypical view of who is a flexible worker and how flexible working structures might look. So, my first request to you is to be a little more Elvis and to begin to 'dream'. To help structure your musings, there is actually a very helpful list of types of flexible working which are defined by the Department for Education and are as follows:

1. Part-time working
2. Job-sharing
3. Compressed hours
4. Staggered hours
5. Working from home

Straightaway we can see that it is not just all about working part-time, although part-time working and job-sharing are often lumped together in a kind of edu- duet or mash-up. It's important if we are to think creatively that we do not bung these two together as, although they do have much in common, there is actually much more possibility and innovative thinking within organising staffing if we keep these as two solo voices. Just to be awkward, I'm going to start with the second on the list: job-sharing.

Job-sharing

This is the equivalent of the duet. A job or role is split between two or more employees and the responsibilities are shared, sometimes equally, sometimes with one taking on more of the contracted hours. Commonly in schools, this is a class teacher job-share with common carve ups being 0.5 and 0.5, 0.4 and 0.6 and more rarely 0.8 and 0.2. This allows for a full-time job to be carried out but shared between colleagues. It is important to note when planning the carving up of the role whether this is going to be an Elton John and Kiki Dee type shared duet with both having equal weighting or whether it's more of an Ironik featuring Elton John performance with one taking the lion's share of the role and one being a 'featured artist'. I've mentioned that this is a common model for class teachers in schools but just as you wouldn't necessarily think of Ironik and Elton John being a usual match, so too should we think far more broadly about the wider potential of job-sharing. I've worked in a job-share in a very successful co-headship and know first-hand how leadership roles are perfectly suited (often more so than a single person in a leadership role) to job-sharing. The benefits of job-sharing will be explored in more detail later, but we must dispel our preconceptions immediately that job-sharing is simply for one particular role or level of responsibility in our organisation. Let's not do an immediate Elvis default vision and instead think and dream much more broadly about the possibilities job-sharing opens up at every level.

Part-time working

So, let's backtrack to number one: part-time working. In short, this is doing a job for fewer than full-time hours. This often gets lumped in with job-sharing due frequently to a lack of vision or innovative thinking or being unknowingly hamstrung by conventional thinking and models. Part-time working offers a myriad of different options and the potential for the creation of new and exciting roles. It is not simply just one fraction of a traditional full-time role. Think of it in food terms as being the opportunity to have tapas, lots of little dishes of deliciousness rather than one great huge traditional plate of dinner. In musical terms, it's like an overture or a medley rather than a single hit. As soon as we start thinking about roles in school being more like tapas then a whole world of new opportunities opens up.

Part-time working is one of the most exciting aspects of flexible working as it allows for the creation of completely new roles. It is madness to me that in the system where the curriculum, its assessment systems, its initial teacher education structures, its school age ranges and its accountability systems have all undergone radical overhauls in recent years, the bulk of our job titles and roles remain unchanged. It's a little like trying to produce the music of Kraftwerk or The Chemical Brothers on a harpsichord and lute. We need to think much less traditionally if we are going to provide the innovation and creative thinking to staff our systems appropriately and respond to the needs of our changing societies and our students. So, part-time can simply mean fewer hours but not necessarily less impact or less importance. One person in my former school who worked part-time but who without the place would have collapsed was our bursar. There is no way on earth we could have fathomed the intricacies of our budget without her expertise but neither did we need a full-time bursar. In addition, we also had a part-time SENCo who used to be full-time but wanted to relinquish the bulk of her role but still use her specialist diagnostic qualification. We were able to retain her talent and expertise and provide an opportunity for another member of staff to undertake SENCo training and become the school's SENCo, which incidentally they also did part-time.

I have also seen great innovation in other schools and trusts where they have newly appointed research or transition leads who are part-time. I am now beginning to see more part-time work at leadership level but this is still rather the Lady Gaga meat dress of part-time working in that it is still very rare and raises more than a few eyebrows amongst those wedded to traditional models. What is important is to bear in mind the opportunities part-time working models present. They are the key to really beginning to shake things up within flexible working as they are the roles which can be the winners of 'Best Newcomer' with the fresh thinking they bring and can be the perfect complement to more established players within the education orchestra. In Elvis terms, they are like when Fatboy Slim did the remix of 'A Little Less Conversation' and brought Elvis to a whole new generation of listeners.

Compressed hours

Compressed hours are a funny one in education. They are where an employee works full-time hours but squeezes or 'compresses' these into fewer than five days. This is a very popular model in the health services

34

and other sectors where a few longer or shorter shift patterns can be worked. The same hours are worked but just in different patterns. This one is a trickier one to manage with a full-time teaching commitment, but it still does provide scope for thinking differently. What is to say that a 0.6 contracted part-time teacher can't deliver all of their teaching over two full teaching days and then use the third more flexibly as non-contact, PPA, management time or for other responsibilities? We need to stop thinking of contracts always as 'days' in that we shouldn't automatically assume that 0.6 is three days of contact time. We could compress the contact time over two and leave the other 'free' for more flexible ways of working such as off-site/remotely. We can also look at the wider staff in our organisations who are not shackled to a teaching timetable when looking at compressed hours. There are so many positions in a school not just teaching and we should aim to afford everyone the equal opportunities to work flexibly, not just those in a particular role or at a particular level. With many schools providing wraparound care and extra-curricular clubs there are myriad opportunities to explore compressed hours for a wide range of staff and as soon as we unshackle ourselves from the numbers on a contract automatically aligning with a specific number of days then we can begin to enact change.

Staggered hours

Staggered hours could be thought of as the sibling or cousin of compressed hours as, like compressed hours, this is deliberate and strategic tinkering with the established norms of working hours. This model is one which has huge benefits for employees who wish to balance caring commitments as it enables them to potentially arrive a little later or leave a little earlier. It is this often small tweak which can mean the difference between a colleague feeling their job is doable rather than completely unmanageable. The ability to do a school or nursery drop off/ pick up with a young child, to travel to visit an elderly relative or attend appointments with a dependent can make such an unseen but hugely important difference to those colleagues who are finding the rigidity of the traditional school hours a real barrier. Staggered hours can be the unsung hero for many employees and employers when trying to strike a balance between the needs of the organisation and the home lives of the employee. Sadly, it is an all too often underused approach to flexible working but in terms of retention has enormous potential benefits.

Working from home

Working from home in the Department for Education guidance is not in the actual flexible working list but is mentioned as an add on; it states that working from home doesn't lend itself to teaching so easily. This now makes me smile when I reflect on the fact that this was so obviously written prior to Covid-19. If the lockdown has taught us anything it is that nothing is set in stone. There is much of our roles that can be done at home which doesn't require us all present and correct in the school buildings at set times. I had initially written this entire book on flexible working prior to Covid-19 and it read more or less like an extended plea for people to understand that it was possible to work from home. Because of the virus, much of the donkey work around that particular narrative has now been done for me and so much has been achieved in the field of remote working and working from home in recent months that I had to completely rewrite the entire book. My work was out of date in the few very short weeks it took for a tiny virus to spin everything we knew about the working from home part of flexible working on its head (as well as our entire lives). I'll expand more on principles of effective working from home in later chapters but, for now, I reckon we all agree to sing from the same song sheet and that we've shown that, as a profession, we can be more than trusted to do a damn fine job of a lot of our role without the need to be sat around a sad and tired plate of biscuits in a badly lit draughty room for hours at the end of a teaching day. There is another way and like Elvis, our working from home approaches have indeed by a global pandemic been *all shook up.*

Questions to consider

Employers	Flexible workers
How many of the five flexible working practices could be found across your organisation?	Which of the five main working practices would be of most interest to you?
When advertising a new role, is flexible working information added to any promotional or advertising material? Is your organisation clear about its approach to flexible working and is this communicated when advertising?	Do you know other workers in your organisation who work one of these five models? What have been their experiences and thoughts about benefits and challenges?
Are all new or replacement roles analysed for their potential to be offered flexibly?	If you are interested in roles both within or beyond your organisation, have you enquired as to whether these could be worked flexibly?
Do you actively explore the creation of new roles which are not necessarily the traditional educational role hierarchy?	If you could work your current role flexibly, would you want to? What would be the benefits or challenges?
Do you encourage as many flexible workers as possible into leadership roles? Do your leadership teams across your organisation represent a wide range of working structures? How many of your most senior posts are made up of flexible workers?	What would be your dream role both in terms of responsibility and working pattern?
How do you communicate what the five main flexible working practices are to all stakeholders? Does everyone in your organisation and associated trusts, boards, governors and so on understand the five main practices? Are they aware of how they could be utilised? How is this discussion facilitated and revisited/reviewed regularly?	

Track four: Wannabe
Spice Girls

'If you don't ask, you don't get.' - Reet Turner

Despite being a proper '90s indie chick at heart and with an encyclopedic knowledge of UK guitar bands of the late '80s and early '90s, there's a special place in my heart for all things pop and most definitely a shrine-like corner reserved just for the Spice Girls. I saw them last year on tour in Coventry, a couple of days before my birthday. I went with my best friend who I lived our original Spice Girls love with back in the '90s. I've never seen so many women of a certain age so over-excited, covered in glitter and reliving their youths all at once in the most tipping Biblical-esque rain in an open-air football stadium. A sea of ponchos revealed thousands of now 40-something, drenched wannabe Scaries, Sporties, Gingers and the now-ironically titled 'Babies'. As the ticker tape, fireworks and lasers battled against the open-roofed and soaked venue, I belted out every song from their back catalogue with the same gusto I'd done the first time around over 20 years ago.

They left their most famous song 'Wannabe' until last and as Mel B did that iconic giggle over the opening bars you just knew the first few lines were going to be sung at top volume by a now almost hysterical army of perimenopausal women, myself included. There was a video I posted on social media from that night where I am just screaming, 'I'm with the Spice Girls!' and twirling around like kid who's had too much sugar. Truth was, it was the Spice Girls' optimism and 'Girl Power' which had been such a refreshing change to the sugary pop offerings of previous years. The cheekiness (albeit very much staged) and the challenging of established norms by the Spice Girls was not just music to my ears back then but balm for the potentially jaded teenage soul full of ennui and angst. The pinching of Prince Charles' bum, the crazy outfits, the cartwheeling on tables, the delight in doing things differently was very much part of my late teens and early 20s cultural zeitgeist. Just as Abba shook things up with 'Waterloo' in 1974, so too did the Spice Girls with their fresh way of challenging everything dusty and 'establishment'.

The fact that they were unafraid to do things differently and ask for what they really, really wanted (see what I did there?!) was one of the most refreshing aspects of their band persona. Twin that with the wise words of my mum at the beginning of this chapter and you have the potential winning formula for beginning to think about flexible working. Many people ask me 'why flexible working?' and my initial go-to setting was to try and collate multiple facts, figures, data sets and carefully crafted case studies to back up my responses. But do you know what that does? That implies that flexible working is something different, special and only for the few – the exceptions – or that it is something which is graciously bestowed upon those who have jumped through sufficient hoops or who have managed to go cap in hand to those who have the power to grant a flexible working request. What it doesn't do is assume that flexible working is normal and shouldn't need to be accompanied by a tonne of persuasion. The fact that the data and the case studies and the facts and figures even need to exist makes my blood boil as it is in my mind akin to Oliver Twist with his 'please, sir' famous line but rather than asking for some more, in the context of flexible working, is like saying, 'Please sir, can I have some less?'

There shouldn't be a need to have to justify the concept of flexible working. It is indicative of those who generally tend to be in the position to grant the requests not necessarily being the same demographics who might need to utilise and benefit from a flexible working arrangement. As I've mentioned, I've worked flexibly on and off since 2004 in multiple different roles. The following chart might only be of interest to my mum who I quoted earlier as it's basically my work timeline, but I've included it as it makes a few important points about misconceptions around flexible working.

You'll see from the timeline that I've worked both full and part-time both pre and post-children. Many people assume that I only worked part-time after I had my children, but I was working part-time hours way before I even met their father! The thing is that I was pursuing other interests as well as teaching and was also renovating my home. It meant that I didn't want to juggle five days per week of teaching with everything else and end up running myself ragged. I remember speaking to my mum and explaining that it was all or nothing in teaching really. You either ended up working full-time or not at all. I remember her pushing me over and over on this point and asking me to explain exactly why that was and then encouraging me to just ask the question. Her mantra of, 'If you don't ask, you don't get' is a common refrain in our family and so I did. I asked the question and it was granted immediately. I went down to four days per week despite being the Year 6 teacher, a lead teacher for the local authority and the maths subject lead. I was lucky enough to work for a very forward-thinking team who despite the school being in special measures, knew that a four-day week contract would mean retaining me at my best whereas the other option was me either burning myself out or just deciding to leave. My mum would've been a great Spice Girl.

You see, I've been lucky enough to be instilled with a lot of what some might call cheekiness, sheer brass neck or 'chutzpah'. My mum and dad aren't university graduates with qualifications coming out of their ears. I'm not from a hugely privileged or privately educated background and was the first girl in my family to go to university. My mum went to grammar school, despite not speaking any English until she was seven, and left at 16. Due to many factors, she was not able to pursue her dream of attending art school. She's an amazingly talented artist who now, in her retirement, is finally honing her gift at her leisure. My dad has never been one for convention either. Finding themselves both out of work and with absolutely no money when I was very young, my dad took the somewhat maverick decision to sell our home and keep half the garden. Despite not being a builder (he had multiple exam qualifications in banking and finance but was definitely not a builder), he read books, went to night school and taught himself how to build our modest family home from the ground up where my parents still live today. He retired in his 40s and helped my mum with her retail business which she also created from scratch. Dad has also done other rather unusual things like – despite living his entire life in the landlocked Midlands – going to evening classes to learn how to sail and read nautical maps and then sailing a boat from the UK all around Europe. Our family holidays as kids were never to anywhere 'normal' or done in the usual ways either. It was a revelation to me as an adult that package holidays even existed! My brother has inherited their risk-taking and entrepreneurial streak and I often joke that I am the only one in the family with a 'proper job', albeit one where I still don't work in a traditional setup – it seems the 'doing things differently' gene is strong in our family. What their combined success has taught me is that you get nowhere by doing the same as everyone else. Whenever I've presented them with a problem due to a system or a specific way of doing something, their answer has always been to challenge it, to ask for what you want, to not assume that there is only one way of doing something. To always ask because 'if you don't ask, you don't get'.

So, when thinking about flexible working requests, we need to channel a bit more of my mum and dad (and the Spice Girls) and start asking for what we want. As employers we also need to be clear what we want. My employers in 2004 wanted to retain their Year 6 teacher and ensure that the school went on to come out of the 'special measures' category.

At no point did I say to them during the request that I was planning on leaving if they didn't grant it; I wasn't planning on holding them hostage or blackmailing them, it was simply a request. It was a bold one too as I didn't really have a reason for it. I didn't have a caring commitment of any sort, I was in good physical and mental health and I was performing well in my job and taking on lots of additional responsibilities. If you'd done a quick scan of the staff at the time, you'd have probably had me pegged as someone hungry for promotion and taking on much more. The thing is *that* is the problem with a lot of our systems, they assume that there is a direct correlation between ambition and doing 'more'. The truth is I was incredibly ambitious, a little precocious and – looking back – probably frankly unbearable (the current me would definitely have a few choice words to say to the old me should our paths ever cross in a parallel universe) but my senior team were savvy enough to know that this correlation is a misconception. Ambition is not about doing more and career progression is not about filling up every waking moment of your life with more work, work, work. It is about providing space to think and develop as well as time tearing around the career track. Just as every great piece of music has a killer chord, a killer note or a beautiful melodic moment, so too are the silence and pauses in between the notes just as important and impactful as the energy of the notes themselves. Think about that pause in the singing in Whitney Houston's 'I Will Always Love You' before she hits that big note and you'll understand exactly what I mean.

So, if an organisation wants to hold onto their staff and really develop their school then they need to be clear about what they really, really want. Do they want staff who are on contracts which don't tally with their home commitments, so they are stretched paper-thin and unable to find the time for reflection and development? Do they want to develop a culture where flexible working is only for the few and not an integral, valued way of structuring working patterns? Do we want to create a culture where staff are fearful of asking the question about flexible working as they have an assumption that it will be turned down or immediately asked for alongside a justification of the 'why' they want it. You see, I know that when I first put in for my flexible working request I didn't really have a 'why' other than I was really busy and a bit tired, but the fact is that most people who put in for a flexible working request already have a tonne of other stuff in their lives. That's the exact reason they're asking for the request in the first place. It's actually why I coined the phrase 'flexible living' rather than 'flexible working' as work shouldn't be what dictates our lives.

Flexible working requests are for people who want to live more flexibly. They're the colleagues already juggling parenting or caring for elderly relatives; they're the colleagues with their own physical or mental health challenges; they're the colleagues who want to pursue other work or study to give them balance, breadth and fulfilment. They are not colleagues who are being work-shy, far from it; they are the ones wanting to stay in the game, who know they have something to contribute, who want to commit and be valued not simply overlooked or overworked because they have a life outside the school gates. The wider the range of lived experiences we can bring to the staff table, the more likely we are to ensure a truly diverse staff voice. If the only voices around the staff or leadership tables are those who can work full-time in a traditional setup then where is the diversity? Why should colleagues who have other commitments outside of school be precluded from being part of the education discussions? By upholding outdated structures and systems not only are we preventing potential innovation, but we are also silencing the voices of staff with a more diverse range of lived experiences. By doing so we are inadvertently assigning privilege to those who do not have caring commitments, who may be a sole carer or parent or who does not have anyone to share the caring responsibilities with, who are in good health, who do not have children or who do not want to pursue any other interests outside a full-time contract. That narrows any discussion around any table and be that one about recruitment or curriculum or pedagogy then any discussion can surely only be all the richer when the voices around the table are varied? I would always advocate, just like the Spice Girls had very different personas, we should look to create our own staff Spice Girls teams. Now let's just check for alongside 'full-time Spice' that we encourage the inclusion of 'part-time Spice', 'job-share Spice', 'compressed hours Spice', 'staggered hours Spice' and 'dialling in on Zoom, working from home Spice'.

Questions to consider

Employers	Flexible workers
How many flexible working requests are submitted each year and how many are agreed? Is this figure the same for roles at all levels of our organisation?	What is the reason for your flexible working request? Caring, parenting, study, health, and so on.
Are conversations around flexible working built into everyone's appraisal/career development/ coaching opportunities?	How would you utilise a flexible working arrangement? What would be the benefits? What would be the drawbacks?
Who decides if a flexible working arrangement is granted or not? What are the reasons for agreement or refusal?	Does your flexible working request still include enough space for you to develop and create balance? How will you continue to develop your professional learning in the request setup?
Are we aware of how many people in our organisation would be interested in working flexibly should the opportunity arise? How does this figure compare with how many colleagues actually work flexibly?	Have you articulated your longer term career goals alongside your initial request?
Are our flexible workers all from a single demographic, e.g. returners from maternity/ paternity or adoption leave?	
What are our leadership teams' views on flexible working?	

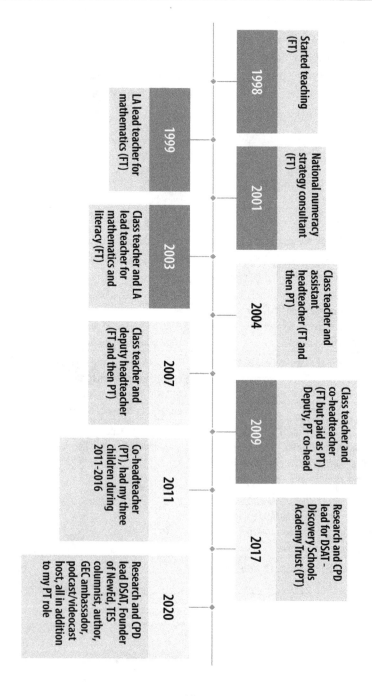

1998 — Started teaching (FT)

1999 — LA lead teacher for mathematics (FT)

2001 — National numeracy strategy consultant (FT)

2003 — Class teacher and LA lead teacher for mathematics and literacy (FT)

2004 — Class teacher and assistant headteacher (FT and then PT)

2007 — Class teacher and deputy headteacher (FT and then PT)

2009 — Class teacher and co-headteacher (FT but paid as PT) Deputy, PT co-head

2011 — Co-headteacher (PT), had my three children during 2011-2016

2017 — Research and CPD lead for DSAT - Discovery Schools Academy Trust (PT)

2020 — Research and CPD lead DSAT, Founder of NewEd, TES columnist, author, GEC ambassador, podcast/videocast host, all in addition to my PT role

Track five: You Can't Always Get What You Want
The Rolling Stones

My mum, who I've already mentioned, is a massive fan of the Rolling Stones. I remember my brother and I buying her tickets to see them live for her 50th birthday not too many years after I was into the Spice Girls first time around. You see my mum has always been super cool and a little bit of a rebel and she'd often listen to the Rolling Stones when I was little. I remember her and my Dad often dancing to them at the parties they would host. Whenever I hear the Stones I now always immediately think of my mum. Despite her insistence that if you don't ask you don't get, she's also realistic enough to know that as the Rolling Stones song title goes, 'You Can't Always Get What You Want' and it is this we also need to bear in mind when we think about flexible working. I've not always had every flexible working request approved.

Although Claire, my co-head partner, and I flexed our days and worked many different combinations of days and contracts throughout the eight years of our co-headship and the five maternity leaves we had between the two of us, there came a time when my home and work situation no longer aligned beautifully anymore. There were a combination of factors including a ridiculously lengthy and frustrating commute route, astronomical nursery fees for two of my children, juggling wraparound school care for my eldest, a husband who worked away a lot and often very unusual or unpredictable hours, my own exhaustion due to absolutely none of my children ever agreeing to sleep a single night through in what was by then five solid years, and the feeling that I couldn't maintain my then commitment to the co-headship role, I had to admit that I couldn't keep up with my already very flexible role. I needed to either leave or reduce my hours temporarily to just one day per week.

The governors who had championed the co-headship quite rightly to protect the school and Claire said that it wouldn't work as I would end up being in more of a consultancy role rather than a true co-headship. I remember feeling a little crestfallen as I was already exhausted and the emotional toll of admitting that maybe I was actually struggling to 'have it all' as mothers – but interestingly never fathers – are so often accused of wanting, was slowly eroding both my professional and personal confidence. I wanted to do a good job; I'd always done a good job. I wanted to champion flexible working, especially for working parents and parent leaders but at this point the burden was a little too much to carry. Three insomniac little ones all aged five and under, a hideous commute, sleep deprivation and the crippling nursery fees meant that something had to give and so when my request to go down to one day was refused, I had to think of something else. I'll admit that at this point I felt a hell of a fraud and more than a little bit of a failure. I was exhausted, I was consumed by the thought I was somehow not as effective as I previously had been and I was terrified of letting everyone down, whether at work or at home. I was so busy trying to spin all the plates, smash all the glass ceilings, fly the flag high for working leader parents that I'd actually ended up absolutely stretched too thin and was temporarily knackered.

It would have been really easy to step out of the game at that point. It would have been really easy to think that taking a career break would solve everything but I knew I had worked too damn hard to do that so if couldn't get what I wanted as the Rolling Stones sing, then maybe I actually needed something else. What I needed was to talk with my mum and dad again. A simple conversation with them convinced me that there was a whole world of opportunity out there and I just needed to create my own luck, use my own networks and think carefully about what I actually enjoy. If you've read my previous book *Be More Toddler* this was one of Dad's chicken soup moments at my parents' kitchen table. I cannot stress the importance of connection with the people who know and love you outside of the education system. The simple question from my dad of, 'What do you want to do Emmy?' sparked a thought that I really loved research and CPD, which I'd got a taste for during my work within our teaching school Alliance and which I'd been doing alongside the co-headship.

I was already writing and delivering the bulk of their NQT programme as well as trust-wide maths training that I'd written during my second maternity leave. I loved working with early career teachers and I realised that much of the day-to-day parts of headship weren't actually giving me the same fire and enthusiastic fizz eight years on which I'd had previously. Don't get me wrong, I really loved that school and its community and it will always be where my educational heart lies but at that time, if I really loved it, I needed to walk away and let someone else have the privilege of leading what is simply a diamond of a school. I decided to ring the CEO of our teaching school alliance after I'd spoken to my parents and ask him for some career advice. It seems that the universe was somehow aligned that day as he told me there was a job coming up in the trust that might be of interest to me. It was only going to be a very small role initially, only about one day a week and was a completely new role of 'CPD and Research Lead' for the trust. I remember I was parked in the car park of a local John Lewis when I spoke to him and I genuinely was stunned as it was like he'd crawled into my head and was explaining my dream job.

I'd gone from thinking I was going to have to maybe leave leadership and teaching as surely there wasn't a one day a week leadership role out there which was about CPD delivery and research but because my mum and dad had once again encouraged me to think, 'If you don't ask, you don't get' I'd ended up hearing about what was to become my dream role. After applying, I interviewed for the position on the same day as my youngest child's first birthday. Not many new(ish) mums have an interview on their baby's first birthday and it was a weird old day having to go from a presentation to a panel and a formal interview to then home to cake, balloons and a tea party. However, I ended up gorging on celebratory cake as I got a call to say I'd got the job, which has turned out to be the most exciting and innovative role that has enabled me to learn so much about the entire sector. I didn't initially get what I wanted with my flexible working request at my previous school, but I did – as it turned out – end up with exactly what I needed.

Now I know that not every flexible working request knock back will have such a fortuitous ending. I know that not everyone is fortunate enough to have innovative thinkers and leaders within the networks in which they work but we must always approach every knockback with the attitude that for every pot there's a lid. I'm a great believer that if you do get knocked back from something that that's simply because of pots and lids. By which I mean that for every pot there is a perfectly fitting lid. That doesn't mean that if a lid doesn't fit then it's a defective or substandard lid. It shouldn't slink off to the back of the cupboard and berate itself for being not 'liddy' enough and try and work out how to be a better lid; it just means that it wasn't the right lid for that pot. Educators are a funny old breed when it comes to knockbacks; we take it so personally. Instead of thinking maybe that place wasn't right for me, we always think we are somehow not right for it. We need to see educational 'fits' as both pot and lid. If we lids don't fit it's not because we're not a good enough lid; we're just trying to fit onto the wrong pot.

One thing I did do with all of my previous flexible working requests was to go with not just the request but also the proposed solution. For my very first request I'd already spoken to the colleague who was covering my PPA time and ascertained that she wanted to do more hours. I'd asked her if I could mention this when I submitted my request and she was more than happy to help. It meant I could go to my senior team with a draft timetable I'd created which mapped how I could continue to deliver continuity in maths and literacy provision for my Year 6 class whilst going down to four days. I'd outlined a couple of options for which days I could have 'off' and what the worked models would look like in terms of impact on the wider work within my subject leadership role and lead teacher work. I'd laid it all out with multiple options and had even done an approximate costing out of the cover for them. I'm fairly sure that because I'd done the heavy lifting in terms of the thinking through of the logistics of my request and presented not one but multiple options then it was one of the key reasons it was granted. No one else in the school without caring commitments worked part-time at that point and definitely no one in a high stakes year group in a special measures school. It was presenting suggestions and solutions as well as requests which was also a key part of setting up the co-headship which I'll expand upon later.

So few flexible working requests are submitted alongside a conversation around possible solutions. And this is not a criticism. I totally understand that many colleagues putting in flexible working requests aren't party to the information about staffing, budgeting, timetabling or other logistical considerations in order to make workable suggestions. Neither is it the responsibility of the employee putting in the request to also think of the solution, especially if they are already stretched thinly between home and work. However, there is nothing to say that solutions cannot or should not be presented as part of an initial discussion. In fact, often the most innovative suggestions can come from the employees themselves who know the ins and outs of their individual role best and can, therefore, see exactly where changes, alterations or new ways of working could be integrated. Employees shouldn't feel like they cannot contribute to the suggestions around what their proposed flexible working arrangement might look like, especially as it'll be them who is having to work with it! So when thinking about submitting a flexible working request, it's important to remember what it is – like the Spice Girls sing – that you really want, and to be like my mum and remember 'if you don't ask, you don't get'. We must also remember pots and lids as we don't worry about not getting what we want – as my mum's favourite Mick Jagger sings – because we might just end up getting what we need instead.

Questions to consider

Employers	Flexible workers
When thinking about new roles or appointing new staff to replace those who are leaving, is there the opportunity to restructure the role and/or create a flexible working option?	What would your ideal flexible setup be?
How are flexible working arrangement requests currently structured? Is there organisation wide guidance or is it at an individual's discretion? Is there an appeals process? How many are accepted/rejected/appealed?	Do you have some alternative models to present/ discuss that would also work for you?
Are we aware of the career aspirations and goals of our teams? How are conversations around these structured? How are they revisited and reviewed?	What are the most important aspects of a flexible working arrangement for you? (specific days, start/end times, opportunities to work from home, etc.) On which could you compromise and which are the most important?
What is the gender balance of our flexible workers? What is the balance of leadership and non-leadership roles that are worked flexibly?	Have you thought of any solutions that may be new or innovative to support your flexible working arrangement request?
Are roles at all level analysed for potential flexibility?	If your flexible working arrangement is rejected, what is your plan? What was the feedback or reasons given for a rejection?
Have you discussed models from other parts of the sector and analysed whether any best practice could be replicated in your organisation?	Do you regularly network with colleagues outside your organisation to support your knowledge of opportunities across the sector?

Track six: Brass in Pocket
The Pretenders

I love Chrissie Hynde. She's fierce and brilliant and, not only that, she has longevity. It's a little known fact that she's the only continuous member of The Pretenders which formed in the late '70s, and in my mind, she's a one woman whirlwind of talent. If you read the story behind the lyrics to 'Brass in Pocket' it's not necessarily about money but about confidence.

Sadly when talking about both money and confidence within the concept of flexible working, both can be in pretty short supply. There is something deeply uncomfortable and ingrained not only in the national British psyche about the vulgarity of talking about money but also within education itself, as obviously teaching in state schools is a state-funded public service and so wages are public money. Align the national discomfort with the widely held idea that teaching is a vocation where public servants are not 'in it for the money' and you have a potential powder keg of writhing embarrassment and inner withering when anyone is forced to talk about wages. The structure of national pay grades in the form of the MPS, UPS and leadership spines go some way to neatly sidestepping any potential embarrassment but with the creation of academies, the introduction of the 'threshold' and the increased accountability relating to performance-related pay alongside the not-always-a-given pay portability of these pay points then increasingly in recent years teachers have had to advocate for themselves when negotiating salary.

When I first started teaching, pay points were awarded seemingly solely for long service and any idea of pay increments being related to performance was never mentioned. I remember distinctly after a few years in the job, my first ever performance management meeting with Gill my former stellar deputy who talked and walked me through the procedure with laser-sharp precision, patience, a huge knowledge of the education system and the opportunities open to me, and then followed this up rigorously with training, mentoring and further reading recommendations. In fact, if you'd set up a video camera back then in the corner of the deserted school library where we'd sat to have our meeting then I'm fairly sure you could have used it as one of those perfect video clips used in leadership training so polished, insightful and effective was Gill's utilisation of the process as a developmental tool for my younger, hungry for promotion and improvement self. In fact, when I ended up going into leadership and started having to performance manage staff, I often reflected on that first meeting with Gill and the subsequent process as I channelled her approach and I tried to 'be more Gill'. This often failed spectacularly though as I'm always telling anyone who will listen that you can't copy someone else directly as you'll just be a bad tribute act like on Stars in Their Eyes. My own performance management meetings therefore were a lot more Emma and you were as likely to hear analogies from Disney films, MasterChef and lyrics from songs quoted as you were to hear extracts from academic texts and the clicking of keyboard presses in neatly typed forms. What I did do (or at least I hope I did) was ensure that every member of staff I was performance managing felt as though they truly were a partner in the process and were not being 'done to' regardless of what role or level they were working in.

In fact, I'll let you into a secret; I used to love performance management meetings. The chance to sit uninterrupted with a staff member and really focus on their aspirations, strengths, achievements and professional learning points was part of the job I really loved. Then following that up with mentoring, coaching, facilitation and training and seeing a real shift in their attitude or practice was a real joy within leadership for me.

To quote another Chrissie Hynde song, titled 'Don't Get Me Wrong', I loathed the associated paperwork with a passion and became like a petulant teen refusing to acknowledge that they have homework to do whenever it came to sorting the typing up of it all, but the actual process? I loved it. However, for many staff, performance management is about accountability. The joint planning of professional learning and the deep discussion around pupil learning and the development of professional skills and knowledge is reduced to a single X-Factor style moment where the employee is just thinking 'stop waffling and let me know if I'm getting my increment or not'!

I've heard of so many badly handled performance management, appraisal or other performance review meetings that, sure as Slade will be in the Top 10 charts at Christmas, there will seemingly always be someone somewhere making a complete ham-fisted hash of the process. The thing is that however bad the process is for full-time staff, for flexible workers it can be an absolute minefield. Many already feel on the back foot as they are simply not there as often as others to be 'noticed' and unless their seniors have made a real concerted, deliberate attempt to ensure their relationships with their flexible workers are as robust as those with their full-time workers, flexible workers can feel much less confident that their senior knows them or gets them. Alongside this they may also feel unsure as to how their senior will handle or respond to the meeting, as they simply don't feel they know their senior either. The relationship and dynamics between performance manager and employee is one based on trust, understanding and knowledge. Flexible workers may be at a disadvantage from the get go as they do not have the full range of opportunities to build this as their full-time contemporaries.

It is a relationship which is all too often overlooked but which was brought home to me during my co-headship. Because I worked part-time and had been on maternity leave, there were staff in the school who I hadn't appointed and who I'd never worked alongside, as they were also part-time but worked on different days to me. That's a very strange relationship initially for both leader and staff member and is one which I had to work hard to ensure didn't have a negative impact. It was also one which was borne out again during our respective maternity leaves where either one of us had to make key staff appointments without the other co-head there. I remember wrangling with one particular appointment during one of Claire's maternity leaves as the panel and I genuinely couldn't reach a decision between two candidates. I remember ringing Claire and talking it through with her for perspective but her saying, 'I can only say I totally trust your decision; I've not met them or been involved in the process so I genuinely can't comment.' There is so much about the importance of trust and relationships that is overlooked in the flexible working narrative at both leadership and wider staff level. Claire trusted my decision because she and I knew each other well, our vision and working practices and knowledge of the school were perfectly aligned and so we could be safe in the knowledge that, in our absence, the other one would make a good decision. Sadly for many flexible workers – whether in a job-share or other arrangement – there is no relationship or confidence 'brass in pocket', or at least there feels as though the pocket may have a bit of a hole in it.

There is also the unspoken but ever present spectre of 'gratefulness' with flexible working. As with the initial flexible working Oliver Twist request of 'please sir may I have some less', there is the whole issue of once one is granted that, somehow we are now wearing a pair of very inflexible golden handcuffs. These handcuffs make us think that we'd potentially never get this deal (either financial or organisational) anywhere again. As many will already be juggling whatever else made us put in the flexible request in the first place, we are so relieved to have found some balance and equilibrium by finding a school which meets our needs, so grateful are we and fearful that we've actually found the work equivalent of a metaphorical unexpected stash of money in the pocket of our dry cleaning (which incidentally is the inspiration behind the concept of the song 'brass in pocket') that we feel we can't ever leave. And so we end up shackled in our self-made professional development prisons, feeling incarcerated by our own flexible working request which we do not believe has any degree of equivalent portability.

From speaking to hundreds of flexible workers across the sector, either in person or on social media, so many of them will admit that they would love a new challenge or a move to another school but feel that they are in these golden handcuffs. I often wonder how many leaders of the schools in which they work are aware of this? What kind of professional fire or intellectual curiosity or ongoing development can be kindled on the damp mildewed feeling of being resigned to being trapped? It's almost as if many of these flexible workers believe themselves to be trapped alone when in actual fact if you had each of these individuals as pins on a map be it locally, regionally or nationally then you would see a sea of pins and maybe that's the point about which we need to start thinking. Flexible working isn't about rigidly boxing people off. We shouldn't fall into a Macmillan-esque trap of peddling a narrative of 'you've never had it so good' to ourselves. Instead, we need to work as a sector to ensure that flexible working and flexible workers do not feel as if they are tied to a role which meets their work life needs but doesn't offer the same scope for career development (including pay progression) as traditional full-time work. By permitting our flexible workers to listen uninterrupted to these negative internal narratives is a dereliction of duty from our educational leaders. Allowing our staff to languish professionally unfulfilled or fearful of raising a point about wanting something more or an equivalent range of opportunities as full-time colleagues is indicative of processes in our schools for developing staff which are not equitable, personalised or carried out within a culture where every staff member is genuinely made to feel valued. At regional, national or strategic level it is indicative of an overly inflexible and outdated organisational infrastructure which as a collective fails to fully recognise or value the contribution that flexible workers have, can and do make to the system. It is one thing to invest millions in advertising to recruit new teachers but where is the investment in ensuring that once in, the system is agile and accommodating enough to ensure that bright talent, wisdom and experience have a full range of options open to them in order to retain them in the profession regardless of whether they're full or part-time? It is a little like constantly putting those brass coins in your pocket but that pocket having a massive hole in it. You're never going to accrue true professional wealth and capital within our education system if you're failing to recognise that some of your most valuable assets are simply falling down the inside leg of your trousers.

The fact that there are case studies needing to be made about the fair payment of TLRs or the development of part-time leadership roles speaks of a system which has a hell of a long way to go in terms of systematically championing fair payment and opportunity for flexible workers. Organisations such as the Chartered College of Teaching, WomenEd, Flexible Teacher Talent, the MTPT project, Shared Headship Network and the GEC are working tirelessly within this space in the sector to champion flexible working at all levels and to show that it can be done as well as providing robust and impartial guidance on issues around contracts, TLR payments and professional development for both employers and employees. What a frustrating place to be in to know that our system needs 'convincing' that flexible working can work. Figures from the 2017 Department for Education report show that we have such a long way to go to catch up with the working practices from the wider world of work and other sectors.

The figures are startling. It appears that we have an awful lot to learn from the wider world of work. Marry these with the fact that women aged 30-40 are the largest demographic to leave teaching and you are beginning to build a picture of why opportunities for a system wide change in approaches to flexible working in education might just be needed to ensure that our flexible workers feel they are championed and do not simply feel as though, like another Pretenders song title, when they begin a flexible working role they are not in their golden handcuffs and simply 'Back on the Chain Gang'.

% of flexible workers	Education	Non-education
Men	8.6	13
Women	26.4	42

Questions to consider

Employers	Flexible workers
How do overall wages/salary points compare for flexible workers vs. non-flexible workers across your organisation? Are the majority of flexible workers in lower paid roles or is there spread across the pay ranges?	How do you ensure that you keep up to date with opportunities both within and outside your organisation? Do you belong to any wider networks, social media groups and grassroots organisations that can help signpost career opportunities?
How are additional responsibility payments allocated e.g. TLRs? How many of these are awarded to flexible workers? Is this proportionate when comparing % of flexible workers vs. non-flexible workers?	Is your CV up to date and does it include both experience and impact? Is it 'application ready'?
How many colleagues apply to leadership positions who currently work flexibly? Are leadership posts advertised as flexible friendly, e.g. open to job-sharing?	Have you considered taking part in career coaching which may be in addition to any coaching provided by your employer?
Does performance management/appraisal/ career coaching include aspirational leadership conversations for those colleagues currently not in a leadership position but working flexibly?	Do you have a clear idea of what steps in your career you would like to take both in the short and the long-term?
How are salary increases decided? Is there the same degree of successful pay progression for flexible and non-flexible workers?	Have we read case studies on successful flexible working arrangements and potentially contacted those involved to discuss transferable elements or to talk through and share ideas?

Employers	Flexible workers
Is there scope across your organisation for career progression opportunities to avoid the 'golden handcuffs'? Are there opportunities for placements, job swaps, shadowing, research, 'acting up', relocation? How are these opportunities flagged up or shared with flexible workers?	How do we communicate our career aspirations and goals to our teams and our seniors? Are we clear about what we can offer as well as what we would like?
How do we ensure that line managers and flexible workers have excellent professional relationships? Is time put aside for KIT days, regular catch up and review meetings, career coaching and development opportunities?	
Are our senior teams aware of the evidence and case studies available through organisations such as WomenEd, The Chartered College of Teaching and the GEC?	

Track seven: Bend Me, Shape Me
The American Breed

I've mentioned before that my mum was very much into music in the '50s, '60s and '70s. She often tells me about getting her first Dansette player in the '50s on which she'd play her collection of 45s. She says she doesn't remember much about the late '70s and subsequent '80s though, as that's when my brother and I were very little and she was drowning in a sea of terry nappies and Infacol. I have a similar musical knowledge gap of the 2011-2018 period which I lived through in a similar fog of Calpol, three reflux babies and potty training. The only musical event I distinctly remember in that period was the opening ceremony of the 2012 London Olympics where a load of school kids sang Danny Boy and Jerusalem and I, in a hormonal sleep-deprived state, ended up sobbing uncontrollably like a braying donkey through the subsequent giant NHS puppetry part and the James Bond and the queen bit for reasons I still cannot fathom.

I do, however, have a very good knowledge of the music of the '60s thanks to my mum's extensive collection of 45s. I remember playing them almost non-stop as a teen and am still a massive fan of mod, northern soul and Motown. (Sorry mum but I never did get into Cliff Richard despite your not unimpressive back catalogue.) There are very few '60s songs I don't know the words to and one of my favourite topics in history to teach at primary is post-war Britain, which I always chose to do through the lens of music. It's through music that so much rebellion, change and rage against established norms comes. Every generation has its theme tunes to help challenge people's current thinking and every generation has its voices who help to articulate exactly what they're thinking and who capture musically a moment in time.

This is a real 'moment in time' for flexible working. The groundswell of support for flexible working practices in schools is gathering pace as the profession haemorrhages teachers at an alarming rate. The world of education begins to look rigid and dated compared to the wider worlds of work and the opportunity for schools, trusts and local authorities to be more creative in their use and deployment of staff increases. If ever there were a time to seize the day then this would be it, so why are so many organisations still dragging their heels instead of sprinting towards and embracing these new opportunities? Well, I'll give you a list of some of the most common things I hear when I ask the questions around flexible working. Let's call them the 'famous five' rather than the '60s 'fab four' seeing as there are five of them, and then let's bust some of these myths shall we?

1. The parents won't be happy. They won't accept it.
2. Flexible working in leadership won't work. You need one person ultimately in charge.
3. Working out the pay is too difficult. There isn't a contract to cover this.
4. The timetable. We simply can't make it work with the timetable.
5. We already have too many part-time staff.

Parents

Right, from the off let's think about actual parenting. Parenting can be seen as the most crucial relationship in a child's life. A child must have a stable, loving and positive environment in which to learn and grow effectively. Agree? Yep? Well, now think that many, many, many of our children live in homes where there are not one but two or more adults.

Two adults with often different – but often-complementary – skills who both know and care for that child equally. No one would argue that a home would be much more effective and function better if there were only one caring parent instead of two. We accept that in our children's home lives there are many models of parenting – some single parents, some in two adult homes, some with shared parental responsibility across multiple different setups and models, but at no point do we have the same argument which we do in a school that one capable person full-time is preferable to two or more capable people together.

If we translate this to flexible working in education then there is nothing to say that the one traditional full-time teacher wouldn't be pretty mediocre instead of automatically equating full-time with being a 'better' teacher. Metaphorically, if you were to offer a parent the opportunity for their child to be taught by two stellar teachers who both work part-time or one OK teacher, I'm fairly sure I know which option they would pick. Also, for very young children, they are often used to multiple key workers and pre-school staff. Nothing magical happens upon a move into Key Stage 1 or beyond. Educators don't suddenly lose the ability to communicate effectively between each other and neither do children suddenly transition from multiple practitioners in a pre-school setting to needing one person and one person alone in Key Stage 1 and beyond.

When Claire and I set up the co-headship back in 2009, we were primed and ready to field oppositional challenges from the parent body and do you know how many we got? None. We got a few queries about who was best to ask about specific things but absolutely no resistance from the community at all. They were generally delighted that the school was to be led by established members of staff who knew the children and the community. So many parents already work flexibly that they are fluent in the knowledge and systems associated with flexible working. So much of our thinking around whether flexible working can 'work' is coloured by our own experiences and biases. Until the children who Claire and I taught as co-heads become adults and parents themselves (our eldest co-head cohort would currently be 22) then in that locality the adult lived experiences will all have been one school, one leader and usually one class teacher. As the current school populations who are attending with co-leadership setups or multiple flexible working arrangements grow into adults then there will be more cultural lived experience reference points for parents.

At the moment, we do not have an adult population who have any significant experience of teacher job-sharing be that at any level. Think about the fact that many young children think their teachers live at school. They genuinely think that their teacher has no life outside the classroom as they are there all day, every day and at every school event at weekends and evenings. When you ally this with promoting a culture of wellbeing, work-life balance and promoting teaching as a positive profession for young people to enter, it doesn't exactly paint the greatest picture. Who would want to do a job where you work so hard you never go home and have to live in a cupboard?

Flexible leadership won't work – you need one person in charge

I cannot disagree with the above statement vehemently enough. Just like the two-parent argument I made in the previous point, this is simply nonsense. Nonsense which eight years of successful co-headship (and two successful Ofsted inspections where the co-headship was praised as being a strength of the school for those of you who may be accountability junkies) proved to be entirely untrue. The insistence on a one school, one leader model is not only outdated but it is unwieldy, often unmanageable in practice, short-sighted and based a lot of the time on the individual egos of those wanting to be in leadership positions.

When you think about the changing nature of the position of headteacher in recent years, especially alongside the reduction in the number of schools under local authority control and the rise of trusts and academies, the assumption that this has brought greater autonomy for headteachers is essentially true, but with it comes huge additional responsibility. If headteachers cast their minds back over the bulk of many of their working weeks they will find that huge swathes of their days are spent poring over anything from building plans, HR issues, missing fence panels, grievances, budgeting, issues with boilers, drains, servers, (insert your most fickle, temperamental and contrary of systems in here – we all have one in our schools), parking outside the school building, resurfacing playgrounds or haggling for reductions in the costs of services.

Each school will have its cavalry of wider specialist support staff to help with these aspects but ultimately each headteacher will be not only juggling the standards of teaching and learning within a school which is their core business but also running a large site, managing finances, reporting to boards, trusts or local authorities as well as managing an entire staff. It is a herculean task and unless the headteacher is ultimately brilliantly supported by specialist staff in specific areas such as buildings and premises, HR, data analysis, middle/senior leadership and finance then the role can be ultimately overwhelming and provide at the very least little time for adequate reflection and evaluation and at worst a completely undoable job. The smaller the school the more keenly this overwhelm is likely to be felt with smaller primary schools often not having the wider pool of expertise from which to pull during the school day unless they have robust links with other schools or professional support networks. The responsibilities of a head do not decrease with the number of pupils either, they remain the same you just have fewer staff and less money to help you with them. This is why shared leadership roles are ultimately the potential jewel in the crown of workforce reform.

Imagine a headteacher who goes into headship after ten years of teaching. This head has a background in maths and PE and has worked predominantly in Key Stage 2 in two schools. You have a total experience bank of two specialist subjects, ten years of experience, two schools and one key stage. Now imagine a co-headship where one colleague has a background in science and maths and the other in English and history. One has 13 years of experience in Key Stage 2 and in three other schools. The other has ten years' experience over two schools in EYFS and Key Stage 1. You have a combined experience of four specialist subjects, 23 years' experience, three key stages and five schools.

The second model brings with it almost twice the experience and knowledge benefits of a one head model. Built-in there is also support, challenge, educational debate, robust evaluation, joint decision making, two perspectives, opportunities to share and contrast experiences. How can this shared set up be seen as inferior to one person on their own?

This is not to say that one person cannot do a good job, far from it, but no one ever seems to assume that one person would not do a better job than two people in a leadership role. The idea of shared leadership still seems to raise an eyebrow and to occupy the default setting of somehow being deficit to a one head model. In an odd humorous moment of the 'universe in alignment' our early days of co-headship coincided with the setting up of the coalition government between Nick Clegg and David Cameron. I was still teaching Year 6 as well as doing the co-headship at the time and I was doing a project around the general election with my class. They thought it the most natural thing in the world for their government to reflect the kind of leadership job-sharing they were seeing in their school and I remember Claire and I joked that we'd got there first and that 'Dave' and Nick were clearly copying us!

I'll leave it up to you to decide whether or not they actually did a good job or instead made a right mess of it or not but the fact remains that the most senior leadership position in the country was not precluded from a form of flexible working job-share. If national government itself can realign its organisational infrastructure and share a leadership role then the argument that individual schools and organisations cannot sort of falls apart. I'll expand more upon what makes for a successfully shared leadership position in later chapters but one important point to make here early on is that of the vulnerability of the solo headteacher/leader. Solo headteachers can be classed as 'lone workers'. They are the only person in an organisation doing that particular job and, therefore, have no colleagues or contemporaries doing the same work with the same pressures, requirements, accountabilities, shared experiences or opportunities for collaboration. They are effectively managing every single other member of staff and their advisors in the form of their trusts, boards or governors are ultimately their seniors to whom they are accountable. Unless these solo heads have a robust and supportive network of other heads and a trust or board or governors who actively understand this and who place the headteacher's wellbeing as an active 'agenda item' for ongoing review and support then that headteacher is the most vulnerable member of staff in the school in terms of wellbeing.

One of the great things about co-headship and co-leadership is that it can neatly sidestep this. Built-in is support and a shared understanding of the role, it's challenges, its triumphs and its flashpoints. There is such relief in knowing that the buck is shared, the can is carried together and that there is no point at which you are ever truly alone. This sharing of responsibility brings with it added confidence to try new things and so can accelerate the pace of development as there is a 'safety in numbers' mindset rather than fear and self-preservation leading to hesitancy and self-doubt. You could argue that a good relationship between a deputy and a head or another similar setup can replicate this but when it's your name and your name alone who is the name on that letterhead, that report or that signature sanctioning something then those are the things that can keep you up at night. Whenever a co-leadership comes across a bump in the road then there are always two of you to navigate it. There are complementary skills, someone to commiserate and celebrate with and someone to point out the detail or perspective you may have inadvertently overlooked and to tell you sometimes that your idea is frankly ridiculous and what the hell are you thinking.

There are people who crave this kind of responsibility who do ultimately want to be the one solely in charge and these kinds of people will most likely do a great job. But they are often pretty few and far between and the deficit number of leaders compared to the number of leadership positions we have in our schools can't simply be filled by these solo leaders. There is so much untapped skill and potential out there, often amongst those professionals who are not the kind of person who wants to be a solo leader. They have the knowledge and the skill but maybe their circumstances or their personality means that they would prefer to share the role. Just as two adults can effectively run a home and a family as a partnership, so too can this translate to leadership at work.

It always seems a little odd to me that we live and organise our lives effectively and predominantly in social groups and partnerships yet when we look to run a school we look to have a single leader. Maybe the time has come to bend and shape the leadership role to fit not with the historically outdated narrative of educational leadership hierarchies but to bring it smack bang up to date with not the equivalent of the 2.4 children historical home narrative but with a much more up-to-date modern family.

Working out the pay is too difficult

I'll agree that working out pay can be a headache. When Claire and I first set up the co-headship there was not even a drop-down menu tab at our local authority payroll centre for 'co-headteacher' and for a few terms we had to wrangle with various incarnations of our play slips until we could be paid appropriately. That is not to say anyone was trying to swindle us, far from it. We had immensely supportive governors who worked tirelessly to ensure that we were paid correctly and that systems were adapted to reflect our new roles.

Initially there were teething problems with merging our deputy head payments and new co-head payments into one payslip. We also set up the co-headship with six days in total of headship to allow for crossover time and to reflect the fact that Claire and I had not appointed two new deputies to replace our roles so were, in reality, doing much more than 2.5 days of leadership each. There were glitches in the system as no one could work out how to pay more than 100% of a headship salary but our governors continued to advocate for us and pointed out how heads in other schools received additional payments for consultancy, NLE/LLE work and inspection and that these were able to be processed and so a way was found around another payroll barrier.

We had to be vigilant in those early days too and became adept at navigating the various codes on our payslips as often, as the system was new, we'd find odd times our pay was 'off' and we'd have to raise this with our local authority who were always helpful and supportive in developing systems to avoid future glitches. There were a lot of automated 'computer says no' gremlins in those early days and we kept the payroll department on their toes as we then added in multiple maternity leaves, KIT days and changed the number of days we worked during the eight years of co-headship. We worked lots of setups including us both working full-time as class teachers and deputies as well as being co-heads at the same time; models of 3+3 days, 4+2 and 3+2 days. We flexed the payroll system and unknowingly proved that there is no payment setup which is too difficult to sort if there's the will, the supportive governance and trust backing who truly believe in the setup and want to secure appropriate remuneration.

It saddens me to read on social media and hear at conferences and events that there are some unscrupulous or unthinking senior teams who use flexible working setups to try and save money. I have heard horror stories of colleagues who have had full responsibility for results and, therefore, 100% accountability for a body of work associated with a TLR but who, because they are part-time, are only paid a proportion of the actual TLR. I have also heard of colleagues being told that there is no way they can apply for roles which are on the leadership spine because a particular organisation refuses to acknowledge that leadership positions can be anything other than full-time. When we think of how discriminatory this is and how downright unfair and disheartening, we can see why the golden handcuffs I mentioned previously can mean that so many colleagues believe the untangling of the established knots of pay progression and pay norms to be the stumbling block for thinking about flexible working. Once again, school and trust leaders must be the ones to demonstrate and actively seek the financial flex within our payment systems.

If Claire and I could do it back in 2009 with zero experience, no case studies and then go on to continually flex the payroll setups to include maternity and KIT and contractual changes almost yearly then sorting out the wages is not a reason to cite as a barrier. If a system like ours back in 2009 was able to accommodate change then it is ready for change. Long gone are the days of sitting with a calculator and poring over an accounts ledger. Our computer systems are nimble and agile and able to be adapted very quickly to accommodate payroll adaptations. It is, therefore, often not a case of 'computer says no' but 'senior leadership says no', which is a very different standpoint.

The timetable

If I had a pound for every time I've heard the timetable argument for flexible working then I would probably be sitting on a beach sipping something out of a pineapple while swinging in a hammock rather than in my home office with a view of a pile of clothes awaiting ironing and a half-drunk tepid cup of tea.

The timetable is wheeled out to be thrown like the globe onto the back of the flexible work argument like Atlas. The fact of the matter is that this is a complete smokescreen. Yes, it's tricky. Yes, it provides, on first glance, seemingly more challenges than dealing with full-time staff but just like those Victorians who thought that if we went above a certain speed on a train then we would all explode or go mad, it is generally a catastrophising assumption. I also feel that those who use the timetable now as an excuse to galvanise their arguments against flexible working are a little like King Canute and the tide. Using the timetable as the tide which cannot be stopped and will, therefore, thwart even the most valiant organisational efforts is false.

There are multiple timetabling software packages out there which can solve most of the thornier timetabling problems at secondary, and at primary there are multiple ways in which classes and cover can be flexed to allow flexible working to be accommodated. A flat 'no' to flexible working requests using the timetable as a reason is a little like the payment argument. It is exceptionally rare to genuinely not be able to find some form of a timetabling solution when the school leaders are wholeheartedly committed to making flexible working work. Yes timetabling is a headache, yes it has budgeting and workload and wellbeing and CPD and training and induction and mentoring and coaching and pretty much everything implications but should not be the sole reason that we say 'flex can't be done here'.

From talking to experienced school leaders with significant experience in planning and timetabling, many point out that yes, flexible working can initially appear as a bit of a headache but if you start with the needs of the school and the students and work backwards from those and the flexible working patterns then it is possible. They also point out and echo a point I often make that those multiple flexible workers provide inherent flex in your timetable. If you have only full-time workers, those workers cannot work any more than full-time. If you have flexible workers then there is potential flex built-in. The good thing about flexibility is that it is *flexible!* If you have three part-time science teachers within your department and then there is a need to provide more sessions of science within particular year groups or subjects then you have three potential people who are able to cover. This is particularly useful if the extra bits you need are not necessarily enough for a full role which you could advertise. Perhaps you only need two extra science sessions per week. This might be a challenge to recruit for outside the organisation but this could work for three potential candidates, who are established team members that know your staff, school and systems, might want to pick up a small amount of extra work. This also works when planning projects such as action research or lesson study. With flexible workers there is the inbuilt flex there for colleagues to either become involved in additional projects or to take on additional teaching session to release colleagues to become involved. Once the flex worker and full-time worker blend are seen as a timetabling benefit then there is huge potential for timetables to be flexed.

If the recent pandemic has taught us anything it is that there is nothing which can't be flexed and done differently. The fact that students could access online learning, that learning could take place supervised by an adult but with the teacher using a pre-recorded session, the fact that learning could be done at different times of the day all help to blow the lid on the rigidity of our fixation on being wedded to a traditional school day timetable. I'm not implying that we had it licked in lockdown, oh my goodness as both a parent and an educator there were some spectacular home and online learning car crashes of which we shall never speak again. It appears that thinking 'this is my moment' when entering lockdown as a parent-teacher was a blithe, ill-informed and over-confident fantasy; what ensued was a lot of hair, teeth and hand wringing, a disgusting amount of caffeine, a lot of Joe Wicks and a capitulation that being a teacher and a parent didn't mean you could teach your own kids despite your impressive array of teaching resources you'd amassed over the years and a completely ridiculous belief that your kitchen table would become a hub of beautiful, calm and purposeful learning whilst you happily zoomed your way through your own work.

Lockdown has shown us that there is potential. There is enormous potential for doing things differently and I look forward to seeing how our learning about learning through lockdown helps to shape our timetabling and curriculum in the future. One thing is for certain though and that is that to embrace the historical setups of old without pausing to think about creative future flexes would be a huge missed opportunity for reform and, like me after day four of Joe Wicks, painful and ultimately tinged with regret.

We already have too many part-time staff

When I was a kid I loved pick-n-mix. I'd take pick-n-mix over a giant chocolate bar any day of the week. I once had an old sweet jar which I'd often keep my haul in until I once foolishly put in an old packet of extra strong mints and tainted the whole bloody lot; there is nothing tasty about an inadvertently minty pink shrimp or a minty cola bottle!

The point is that I loved the variety of pick-n-mix, the different tastes, textures and the fact that you could have as much or as little as you wanted. It's the same with staffing. What we need to build in our schools is the ability to respond to change as well as the provision of excellent service. With this in mind, there is no such thing as 'too many part-time staff' but what we're actually saying instead is 'our communication systems and training are a headache as we can't seem to fathom how to get everyone together on the same day to communicate'. When we break down what we mean when we say we have too many part-time staff, we would be hard pushed to pinpoint an actual detrimental effect on the individual classes taught by flexible workers or a negative impact on pupil outcomes or quality of teaching. The barriers are all too often not the quality of teaching but the inflexibility of the communication and training systems associated with our staff. Frequently staff meetings, staff briefings, parents' evenings, staff training and INSET days are cited as the barrier to having more part-time workers. If we could flex these then we could accommodate as many part-time workers as we wanted. Flexible workers are not like chlorine in a swimming pool in that they are a necessary toxin to be tolerated but then at a certain point they become too toxic for the overall environment. They are pick-n-mix.

I'll write more about the absolute organisational benefits of having multiple flexible workers in future chapters but for now, we simply need to stop seeing them as a minority which can be tolerated and accommodated up to a point and instead see them as a possibility to retain and develop key staff and new systems. Again the pandemic has highlighted the myriad ways in which our old organisational argument that we must all be present and correct in the building at the same time for anything meaningful to happen has been overturned. As with timetabling, the time is now to shake up that bag of pick-n-mix and not let it get polluted with a load of outdated old mints.

There are so many easy arguments against flexible working that you can chuck into the debate but few come from a tried and tested evidence base which is centred around research, hard evidence and actual facts. Most are based on assumptions, biases and a 'flexible as deficit' model. If we accept this and try to plough on with the systems, infrastructures and organisational strategies that we have always had without proper investment into the analysis of the actual effects and pupil outcomes associated with flexible working then we are doing little more than being those Victorians who expected people's heads to explode if they went above 40mph on the London to Glasgow. Just as our musical taste and musical listening devices have developed in the decades since my mum was listening to her 45s in the '60s, so too should our educational systems. It could be argued that music today is not as good as it once was but if we look to Glastonbury which was sadly cancelled this year due to Covid-19, there are multiple stages for performers both established and new. The tens of thousands who gather to watch classics like Dolly Parton or Neil Diamond are the same ones who dance to Stormzy, Kylie or Ed Sheeran. As The American Breed, who title this chapter, say, 'Bend me, shape me'; the time is now to reassess our approaches to flexible working to reflect the fact that we don't want to be trying to teach in a digital society on the equivalent of my mum's beloved '60s Dansette.

Questions to consider

Employers	Flexible workers
Of the 'flexible famous five', which would be the greatest challenges to your organisation? Who is most likely to resist or support any changes in these five areas?	How could we present our case within each of the five areas? What would be the benefits of us working flexibly within each of these and where might the challenges be?
Have we thought through the implications of each of the five areas and audited our thinking and attitudes to each of these within our senior and leadership teams?	Have we explored case studies within each of the five areas to see how other colleagues have overcome similar challenges?
What solutions to the five can be generated?	How can we use our experiences during the pandemic/lockdown to present innovative solutions or cases for changes in working practices?
What lessons can we take from lockdown working practices to look at rejuvenation of the five areas or to approach with fresh eyes?	Have I connected with colleagues in wider networks or other aspects of the sector to collate examples of how they have addressed these challenges? Could I use their experiences to help shape my own working practices?
Have we explored how other organisations (including outside education) have worked around solving issues relating to the five areas?	
Have we explored our networks to see how other organisations within education have tackled issues around the five areas?	
Have we explored case studies and examples of best practice within each of the five areas and especially within leadership and the five areas?	

Track eight: Don't You (Forget About Me)

Simple Minds

Not many people know that the '80s anthem 'Don't You (Forget About Me)' was turned down by Simple Minds on more than one occasion. In fact, it was turned down five or six times by the band before the songwriter, Keith Forsey, persuaded the band to take it on. Not unlike so many flexible working requests, it too was initially received somewhat grudgingly and only then finally accepted for a trial because of the tenacity and persistence of Forsey who genuinely believed it could work. It went on to be one of the most iconic songs of the 1980s and was included in the soundtrack to another '80s cultural classic, the coming-of-age film *The Breakfast Club*.

When I heard about Forsey's persistence, I admired the way he had continued to try and persuade Simple Minds that the song could work. He truly believed he had something which could be successful, flying halfway across the world to present it to them one last time before they accepted it. He also presented it not as a *fait accompli* but with enough unfinished parts to allow Simple Minds to put their stamp on it. There was a real partnership between the bones of his song and their final polished version of it. It is this partnership in creating something new and that those setting up new flexible working arrangements could

77

learn much from. The title itself has so much from which we can all learn. Once a flexible working arrangement is in place there is much that still needs to happen. To make the relationship work and to make the arrangement a smash hit there are new practices and approaches that both employer and employee will need to enact.

The biggest shift for me going from full-time to part-time in any organisation is that feeling that somehow you're now on the outside of a circle and playing catch up. Anyone who has ever arrived at a meeting, a party or a social gathering of any description late will recognise this feeling. It is the feeling of somehow not being part of something, having missed something (sometimes that's the opening comments of a meeting, a course of a meal, the introductions and updating pleasantries of the group, or the first few drinks on a night out). It is a weird feeling which, despite how the rest of the meeting or gathering goes, is still a little hard to shake. It's a little like when someone mentions an 'in' joke of which you were not part or all discuss a TV programme you've never watched. It's not that the group are being rude or uninviting or deliberately isolating you but it's a feeling which is present nevertheless.

Being part-time is hard. It might seem an easier option but we grossly underestimate how much information flows around our organisations and how much of the communication of it is unplanned, incidental, reactive or on the fly. It means that for those who are not there all the time, despite being kept in the loop with the same group emails, calls or notices, they can miss out on the more informal sharing of information and this can end up in a situation which is awkward for everyone where the flexible worker feels isolated or on the back foot and others just assumed they knew the information and unknowingly left them out. This can be everything from not having as much time to sign up for a staff night out or being involved in the consultation about the potential venues for this, to not being sent notice of vacancies or positions when on maternity leave or away during a period of ill health. However, schools are usually pretty good at the statutory or 'big' stuff.

It is rare that schools genuinely and deliberately fall foul of not informing colleagues about things which have a legal ramification relating to employment. This is great and should be commended but the smaller stuff is often the stuff which has a huge impact on whether a flexible working arrangement feels to both employer and employee, whether it is actually 'working'. When anyone has a period of absence due to ill health, however small, or when colleagues return from a period of leave there are often 'return to work' meetings and 'KIT' (keeping in touch) days. There is already a recognition that after an absence from the organisation there is a necessary period during which information needs to be shared and plans discussed for the employee to hit the ground running and feel supported and effective in their return.

When I think about some of the weeks I have gone back into roles where I have been 'off' on my non-contracted days, I can feel like the whole world has shifted on its axis and I'm playing a very rapid game of catch up. This used to bother me. I used to think that I needed to be on top of everything immediately and that somehow not knowing was a sign that I was not very good at my job or somehow being burdensome if I asked for additional clarification, but by doing this I was putting the burden of communication solely one-sidedly and on myself. What I have learnt over the last 14 years working in many flexible roles is that generally if you did *really* need to know something, someone will have told you. If you don't know something, if you ask, someone will tell you. What you shouldn't do as an employee is spend a disproportionate amount of your time running around trying to piece together information from multiple sources like some kind of amateur sleuth during your contracted days whilst everyone else is not doing that and is just getting on with their job of work.

The more time we spend trying to prove that we're totally on the ball and know everything, the less time we spend doing our actual jobs which is not a good use of our time. I found that the world does not collapse if you say, 'Oh, I wasn't aware of that; thank you for letting me know', rather than 'I'm so sorry, I didn't know.' It's this shift from apologising for not having been let into the party to simply acknowledging that you weren't aware but now you are that is a small but significant shift in the flexible working narrative too. If it's something you genuinely need to be made aware of and nobody has told you then that's not something for which you should be apologising. If it's something someone told you weeks ago but you haven't read the emails and, therefore, probably should have known it then that's a different matter.

If Covid-19 has taught us anything about communication it's that (my god) we do a lot of it in education and it's helped to highlight how much of it is incidental too. The fact that all of a sudden, multiple staff Zoom calls were eating into hours and hours of staff's days at all levels soon highlighted that actually, as a staff body, we talk a hell of a lot, be that via email, a quick trot over to someone's desk, a word over coffee or a lean in the doorway and a chinwag. We also realised the way we used to communicate much of our information was hugely inefficient and even more so when we tried to wedge it into Zoom or Teams calls. Many leaders realised that agendas needing tightening, meetings needed much more clarity and focus, and the timings of them needed to be much shorter as colleagues began to experience digital fatigue. During an online meeting, we feel the need to maintain eye contact much more than in a traditional meeting. We feel rude if we look away to sip a drink or write a note. We feel we need that fixed, focused, slightly manic 'I'm listening' grin with the sage nodding of the head and the getting to grips with the new social conventions of who speaks/mutes/unmutes where and when. This places much greater cognitive demands on us than in a traditional face to face meeting and, despite the added comfort of potentially attending in pyjama bottoms or trackies (don't tell me I'm the only one who was half business, half slob during lockdown), we really are more tired after an online meeting than in a face-to-face one.

My trust during lockdown quickly became very adept at streamlining meetings – sending pre-reading out in good time, keeping meetings incredibly short, focused and always recorded to watch back at a later time for those who couldn't attend directly due to the multiple demands placed on us all in lockdown. Meetings also had to replace all the incidental communications which occur during the usual working day and so additional WhatsApp channels and teams group chats replaced the coffee machine chinwags and the desk-side drop-ins. One thing I found about this was that I felt much more connected to my teams and colleagues during lockdown than I did in my usual part-time role in the trust. Because I am the only one in my organisation doing the role I do, I am potentially a 'lone worker' and there is the potential to feel very much out of the loop. However, the additional communication channels opened during lockdown meant that not only was I talking to my colleagues much more both formally and informally, but also that because meetings and communications were happening much more frequently on a digital format and being recorded, I was accessing both the ones related to my job and some which weren't directly related but which gave me huge beneficial insight into the wider work of the trust.

I learnt so much about the roles of others and, as a result, I became involved in some projects which I may not have had it been for the traditional communication methods. My trust was also excellent at ensuring everyone felt connected not only to work but to friendship. Additional quiz nights and digital family evenings replaced the usual work social outings and get-togethers for staff. Senior staff made a real effort to contact all staff to check on their wellbeing, not just in their ability to carry out their job but as a real human connection for those strung out with caring responsibilities or those facing lockdown alone. It was also hugely reassuring to see senior colleagues on calls with babies and toddlers on their knees, others with needy and very intrigued pets, and some with accidental interruptions from partners or children or an Amazon delivery! It was a glimpse of 'we're all in this together' and I believe for many colleagues, a real-life lived experiment of the flexible worker who is juggling other life demands. We often wish that someone else could walk a mile in our shoes to truly understand our situations;

many of our leaders have walked more than a mile during lockdown having to juggle work and their households or have seen first hand through the lenses of our computers the backdrop of life against which we are normally carrying out our work commitments.

It has become obvious to so many leaders that there is much more work around facilitating and streamlining effective communication which can be carried out, not only for flexible workers but for everyone. The fact that we have had an actual glimpse into everyone's lives via their home offices, kitchen tables or settees has meant that some of the edges have blurred and the focus has softened. I was on one Zoom call over lockdown where one of the participants said that she may need to step off to go and breastfeed her twins and another where a senior colleague's toddler daughter spent some time sharing her crayon pictures with us whilst sitting on her parent's knee during the call. Considering I've had everything from skips being delivered, hungry pre-schoolers and Barbies with tangled hair interrupting some of my own online calls, all this can only help to add to the picture of what some of the challenges around flexible working are.

You see, the thing is that what we can't expect our flexible workers is to be paid a part-time wage and to be up to speed with full-time information. If we are to embrace a flexi culture then the ad hoc nature of a lot of our communication needs a radical shake-up and a hell of a lot of tightening. What many of us have learnt during lockdown is that it is nigh on impossible to get anything meaningful done or anything requiring more than two available brain cells if you're already juggling the caring of small children. It doesn't matter whether you try and schedule a meeting or a work slot for naptime or some kiddy screen time, they will be the exact moments they refuse to nap or the Wi-Fi will crash or the remote will disappear. In fact, there is a universal direct correlation between how important your online meeting or your urgent email is and the likelihood of your charges doing the exact opposite of what you want or need them to do.

What employees of flexible workers have hopefully realised is that not only are workers flexible but so are most deadlines. I feel so many of us have learnt that 'done' is better than perfect, which has long been one of my favourite mantras, and that nothing magical happens at 5 or 6pm. By which I mean that because this is often 'close of business' for most email deadlines but that timing just happens to coincide with 'the witching hour' – anyone with a child will tell you these are the hours in which the wheels come off the day entirely and you're wrestling hungry and overtired children through tea, bath and bed. Most parents of young children probably have time to gather their thoughts again around 8pm and this is when I know I often get a flurry of direct messages, WhatsApps, emails and texts from my colleagues in various roles across the sector who have small children. For these colleagues, it's usually radio silence and all hands to the pumps anytime from between 4-8pm. Having more notice and flexibility around submission times for work is a huge step forward for many flexible workers. They may already have heard about information relating to work somewhat 'late' due to ineffective initial communication systems, have fewer working days in which to complete it and then less 'spare' uninterrupted time at home.

I genuinely feel that so many of my colleagues who have had to juggle their workload around the lockdown, their own family commitments and home-schooling have had a crash course in just how difficult it can be for anyone to get anything meaningful done at home if home is full of dependents. The thing about flexible working and the pandemic is that what we think of as flexible working wasn't what the lockdown model was, but it did shine a light on was how unmanageable expecting flexible workers to work on their 'days off' and react to deadlines immediately can be.

We shouldn't forget (as the title of this chapter suggests) that when our workers are not in our organisations, they are not necessarily paid to be 100% full-time 'on'. Yes, they should be available for the hours associated with the effective discharge of their duties but these hours should be flexible (unless forming part of directed time). For me, this has meant that on a couple of mornings in a usual week when my eldest two were at school and my youngest was at playgroup, these would be the times I would catch up on my work and do my equivalents of the 'late night in the office'. This meant my time was much more productive as it was uninterrupted; I could schedule actual calls or meetings and tell people with confidence that I'd be available and be able to give people my full attention. These times were not always used for work. Often they were used for the drudgery of day-to-day life such as online banking, laundry or dental appointments but what they were were two small sections of time where I could get stuff done and focus. This is flexible working. This is managing diaries. This is ensuring there is a clear delineation between home and work lives and not a pandemic-induced blurring of the two resulting in some constant boiling pressure cooker of a home and work soup.

Now some people might say that I shouldn't be doing work on days for which I'm not paid. Some might say I'm being taken advantage of but I'd say no. As a teacher and leader, I often pulled late nights, planning at the weekends, evening events, summer holiday days setting up my classroom or meetings with colleagues to do joint or strategic planning. I don't necessarily need to do that now in my role but I do need to read, network, study and connect with other educators in similar roles. I do this in a very strategic and measured way. In the teachers' pay and conditions (the type of contract on which I'm employed), there is a rather woolly paragraph about directed time and then a bit which mentions any other hours that are necessary to carry out the role. It is this bit which I utilise during my two mornings a week if necessary. What I don't do anymore is spend seven days a week in a mass panic that I can't respond to things immediately. I simply put them on my Tuesday or Wednesday morning list and deal with them then.

I'm also very fortunate in that my direct line manager, our deputy CEO, will call me if it's something really urgent and he is incredibly adept at ringfencing my time 'at home' and that of other members of staff who are part-time workers. I know that a key part of my current role being so successful is that he is acutely aware of the concept of fairness and he often speaks of the need to 'protect my time' and 'be mindful of your wellbeing', as well as ensuring I receive any additional overtime payments for any significant additional projects. I couldn't ask for a more aware direct line manager and there are many senior leaders that are managing flexible workers who could learn an awful lot about best practice from him.

Regular meetings with him to catch up and go through my diary and commitments are a key part of how he helps to manage my time. He'll often ask me to send in my diary for the next few months and we'll meet to adjust my workload and pencil in any future projects or developments. He's also brilliant at being focused during these conversations and never assumes that I'll know things, attending the meeting brilliantly prepared (far more so than me) with an overview of things he needs to update me with from the wider work of the trust which, although may not relate directly to my role, help me to understand conversations I may overhear, meetings I may have some part in, or how what I'm doing fits in with the bigger picture. Never do I feel as if these meetings are rushed or burdensome for him. Sometimes they are face to face or over the phone but they are always timely and useful for me to see exactly how what I'm doing fits in with everything and everyone and gives me a chance to discuss any challenges or achievements, as well as just planning my diary. It is a great skill of his to make someone feel both listened to and valued when that person is as part-time as I am in the trust, as despite often doing additional projects, I am on a very part-time 0.2 contract. Nevertheless, due to the skill and commitment to flexible working shown by my senior team, I am made to feel less like an awkward outlier and more like a guest artiste! It is testament too to the ethos across the organisation that all colleagues across the central team and our schools are just as supportive. There is never a rolling of an eye that I'm not in or that my small role is somehow not impactful or valued – quite the opposite. Since I work with lots of diverse groups across the trust, it comes as somewhat of a surprise to many of them that I'm not actually full-time.

I think often of a keynote speech I heard delivered by Laura McInerney a few years ago at a leadership conference, not long after I'd joined this trust, and it was like someone had jolted me with a thousand volts when she made her point. She said that too many people in teaching go part-time because of workload and that they use their unpaid time to do the associated catch up work for their job. They were then effectively taking a pay cut for doing a very similar amount of work. If we are requesting flexible working hours then in the associated additional work, our line managers must also not forget that there needs to be an adjustment in the associated additional work. If we are expecting some of our part-time flexible workforce to carry out the same amount of additional work as our full-time workers we need to be sure that this is both fair, proportionate and, most of all, necessary.

It is this mindfulness and not 'forgetting' about the demands and pulls on our flexible workers alongside the potential for them feeling somewhat out of the staff loop which is one reason flexible working can be viewed as problematic by some. However, it can be made as simple as not 'forgetting', by which I mean not forgetting that the worker exists in the first place, both in terms of employment and socially. As I have mentioned, schools are pretty good at not forgetting the legal stuff, such as the advertising of vacancies and promotion opportunities, but are we as good at remembering to not always schedule social events such as staff buffet lunches, assemblies of thanks or parents' evenings so that part-time and flexible workers don't feel as though they're always missing out?

We must also be mindful of not forgetting what made them ask for that flexible working request in the first place. This is not to say that under no circumstances should a parent employee ever be sent an email with a 5pm deadline and every leader should pre-empt the sending of an email by conducting a thorough analysis of every worker's home circumstances. I know of an experienced and very capable leader who was asked to analyse a very significant amount of data and produce a detailed report by a Monday morning deadline. This is not an unusual request but this leader worked part-time Monday to Wednesday and was sent this request at 4pm on a Wednesday. It is this lack of awareness which makes flexible workers feel as if they are being burdensome and can reveal a lack of awareness by some employers. Most flexible workers feel in this situation that they should somehow be able to shoehorn the work into the timeframe and meet the deadline and, on occasion, there are always exceptions or emergencies which do necessitate a kind of 'all hands on deck' approach (which I'll talk about more in later chapters) but this should by no means be the norm. Being aware of what days people are paid to work on and then adjusting deadlines is courteous. Also, not dropping huge project deadlines with very tight turnaround times and instead including reasonable response and completion times shows an organisation that is much more strategic, in control and less reactionary. The academic year is (usually) very predictable and has a well-understood ebb and flow to it. I am wincing as I type this as we have all just come off the back of the least predictable year we have ever known but 'usually' there is an awful lot more predictability to the flow of work across an academic year and so there is an awful lot more potential to be more measured, well planned and strategic with our sharing of deadlines.

As Claire and I navigated our years of the co-headship, we increasingly became much more strategic and less 'Mario Kart' with our workloads and deadlines too. Once we had been around the leadership track once, we knew the lie of the leadership land. We knew what needed doing when and where and, subsequently, could allocate our time and our staff's time much more effectively, rather than spinning off and crashing at every turn of each term before revving up and roaring off to the next unexpected bend in the diary. Not having an overview and feeling out of control of your diary, like Mario Kart, is a potentially very stressful place to be in. When you're then trying to flex your work too you need to have an even better view of what's on the horizon and employers need to be aware of their drivers and who may have missed the odd signpost. Checking in with colleagues cannot be overestimated in terms of importance. I talk a lot in my previous book about 'checking in not checking up' and for flexible workers this is crucial. Feeling part of a team can be a challenge for a flexible worker as they may not have anyone in a similar role or balancing similar challenges to them.

Actively finding a 'buddy' as well as a mentor on the staff is hugely important. Although you don't have to find your BFF at work, it is healthy and helpful to have someone on the staff who you genuinely like and get on with. These people may be flexi or they may be full-time but if you have at least one friend at work then the likelihood is you won't have to go searching for as much info as you would without one. It's also hugely important to have one person at work who is your buddy and your cheerleader. Having someone to advocate for you, especially in your absence during times when you're not there, helps to oil the wheels of conviviality and communication. This can be anything from someone mentioning on your behalf that you're free on a Thursday for staff nights out to someone sending you a quick text reminder that it's staff photos in the morning so don't forget to wear something you don't mind being immortalised for the year in! I've always been lucky in that I've always made friends at work. In fact, two of my closest friends and godparents to my children are friends I've met through work. Nonetheless, I always work hard at forging positive relationships too. It's harder for people to 'forget' colleagues either accidentally or deliberately if that colleague is always positive, approachable and friendly. Even though I'm very part-time in my current role, my trust always make me feel as though I'm as valued and included as my full-time contemporaries and I'd like to think that they'd say I was always positive about flexible working and worked hard to ensure that I was up to date, positive and part of the team.

So as the artist of this chapter's name suggests, it's not all that hard to consider our flexible workers and to begin to rethink some of the ways in which we approach our communication systems. It is really pretty 'simple' and is just a case of ensuring our flexible workers don't feel the need to sing like Jim Kerr and implore us to 'don't you, forget about me!'

Questions to consider

Employers	Flexible workers
Is there an employee flexi map which has collated and displayed an 'at a glance' overview of when all staff are in? Can this be broken down into teams, groups, faculties, key stages, etc., to enable other leaders across the school to have an overview of flexible working patterns? Is this model used to inform the planning of meetings, training, briefings and school events such as parents' evenings?	Have you communicated your availability regarding communications? E.g. set out of office automatic replies to emails, mentioned to line managers that if they do need to contact you then a particular time is usually good?
Has there been an audit of additional tasks carried out or are part-time staff expected to complete 100% of the work or attend 100% of training in line with full-time staff? Who audits these tasks?	Do you actively form positive relationships with members of staff across the school? Are you consistently positive, approachable and proactive?
Are there regular face to face (online or in person) opportunities for catch up and diary management for flexi workers? What systems do you currently use to communicate information to all staff?	Are you able to get involved with the wider life of the school? Attending events, social staff gatherings? If not all, are there some with which you could become involved?
How could meetings and communications be refined and targeted more effectively? How soon before the meetings are pre-reading, supporting documents and agendas sent out? Does the timing of the sending of these allow for all workers at access these on contracted work time or are part-time workers expected to access these on their non-contract days? How could communication be refined in order to ensure all colleagues have adequate prep time?	Do you have a strategy for 'catching up' with info from your days off? Is this formal or informal Could you suggest a schedule of regular catch ups with line managers for diary review and news updates?
Are meetings recorded and stored with access for flexi workers? How can flexi workers access meeting minutes and actions in good time? Who could they go to for any additional information?	Is it possible to access recorded meetings, minutes or online training at other times? How might you integrate this into your schedule?

Employers	Flexible workers
Is there a designated senior contact for all flexi workers to discuss workload and diary planning? How are these meetings structured – is there a specific format?	

Track nine: Walk This Way

Aerosmith and Run-DMC

One of my favourite ever moments from my children being at school was my middle daughter's nativity. Now if you've read my first book *Be More Toddler* you'll know that she is a tiny little scrap of a thing, me having had the pregnancy of nightmares with her and then her being early and poorly for the first few months. You'll also know that what she may lack in size, she makes up for in sass, resilience and a fierce determination. So when she was cast as a Wise Man/King in her Year 1 nativity I was intrigued. When I arrived to watch her, she was half the size of her kingly contemporaries, her costume of velvet gown and wonky crown simultaneously trailing on the ground and falling over her eyes. However, once we reached her scene I sobbed not only with the usual heady mix of pride and general parental overwhelm but also with hilarity at the wit and wonderful casting decisions of her teachers. You see, my little middle one is so fierce and such a great dancer she makes Beyoncé look like an uncoordinated wallflower. As the kings and their associated camels and courtiers stood to enter the stage, Aerosmith and Run-DMC's 'Walk This Way' came blasting out of the speakers and my little dot led them onto the stage, past the child holding the giant star on a broom handle, and proceeded to bust out the most spirited and unexpected performance I think anyone had ever seen.

This tiny scrap of a six year old with her blonde pigtails sticking out from under that crown made the Run-DMC crew and Aerosmith look like mere amateurs in the attitude department. It was a moment of hilarious casting and a brilliantly witty backing track. For a short moment, this little dot got to showcase something unexpected and new and smashed it. Her teachers had been unafraid to tinker with tradition and, as a result, I and so many of the other parents adored it. The element of surprise with the song choice and then the subsequent dancing meant that what could have been another version of the same old story became something brilliant and memorable, which gave one very small girl a very big moment. The lyrics might leave much to be desired in terms of complexity (and feminism) but you can't deny that it's iconic. The story behind the collaboration goes that Aerosmith had been historically successful but had hit somewhat of a creative and monetary slump. The collaboration was initially not particularly relished by either side but, once in the studio, they knew they were onto an absolute winner. What I loved about this is not just the fact that the collaboration between the two very different groups was unexpected but that the accompanying video demonstrated this through its imagery of literally smashing down the walls between the two groups which resulted in a brilliant joint performance.

Back when Claire and I set up the co-headship, it wasn't anything either of us had intended to do. Our headteacher had left mid-year and, as deputies, either one of us could have offered to step up. However, our circumstances were not ideal. I was about to start the first of what would turn out to be nine rounds of IVF and Claire had not at that point begun to study for her NPQH, which at that time was a prerequisite for headship. Neither of us had headship on our radar at that particular point, nor were we really in a position to take on the role solo. I remembered having read a DfE document about a school which had done a co-headship and Claire and I spoke to our governors about the potential of doing this at our school. The governors were overwhelmingly supportive and after we had shared the DfE case study document with them and outlined how we thought we could carve up the role and still maintain our full-time class teaching commitments in Year 2 and Year 6 then the co-headship was born.

Neither of us at the time thought that we were doing anything groundbreaking or different or particularly interesting in terms of structure, we were simply getting on with a job of work which needed doing. It is only in more recent years that people have begun to comment on how groundbreaking we were and how much 'grit' and determination it must have taken to do something different from the very well established norms. We were invited to speak at a BrewEd with the theme of 'grit' but we chose to use it as an acronym for 'Going Rogue, Innovating Together' as this more accurately described in our minds what we had done. We hadn't deliberately smashed anything or been groundbreaking – looking back now we just feel we had innovated a little. We had simply looked at a situation and offered what we thought was a workable and sensible solution. It helped that Claire and I already had a history of working together, both as class teachers and as the school's two deputies. People were used to seeing the two of us as a united front and we knew each other's working practices and thoughts on things almost telepathically. It was rare we ever had to check something with the other one before making a decision even before the co-headship as 99 times out of 100 we agreed. Our view of education was very much aligned and we were both dedicated to serving the children and their communities as best we could through the provision of an excellent curriculum delivered with warmth, kindness and humour.

The strapline we developed for the school of 'Developing Responsibility, Caring about Achievement' encapsulated for us the importance of ensuring our children became independent and aware, as well as us recognising that achievement was underpinned not only by excellent teaching but the care, warmth, humour, safety, understanding and kindness that a school environment should provide for all of its students and their families. Because we were aligned in our views on what the 'big thinking things' were, then the day-to-day decisions were really easy to divvy up. Our skills, background and experiences were also – like Run-DMC and Aerosmith – very different but ultimately complementary. My specialisms are in science and maths, Claire's are English and art history.

She has huge experience in Key Stage 1 and the bulk of mine in Key Stage 2. She excelled at data, finance, assessment and governance; I was a self-confessed teaching and learning CPD geek. We were the Jack Sprat and his wife or the yin and yang of education leadership. Our backgrounds and experience may have been very different but our alignment on the big stuff meant that it worked. Just as Run-DMC and Aerosmith have their own individual parts to the song, it's the joint parts that are the real success story where their different but complementary styles make it a song we cannot forget. It was not without its challenges though.

Convincing people from different groups that co-headship could work had mixed results. The staff and parents were overwhelmingly positive as were the wider community and our governors but it was (interestingly) some established school leaders who raised their eyebrows the highest and asked the question, 'So, how does that work... exactly?' Of course, there were some forward-thinking school leaders who championed the model and some who even replicated it in their schools and trusts, but there was definitely a swathe of existing school and education leaders who were more than a little sceptical. It also still infuriates me that we never did challenge those heads who referred to us as 'the girls' (we were in our late 20s and early 30s when we first set up the co-headship), who consistently muddled our names and used them interchangeably, or who made those non-committal thinly veiled digs of 'oh, how interesting, how... unusual'. We were determined to make the co-headship work, especially during a challenging first Ofsted where I had been back from maternity for 42 days and Claire for 14. We were resolute in showing that the school had not regressed and instead flourished during the co-headship and it was actually the fact that there were two of us to support each other during this process that made what could have been an extremely challenging time for a solo head feel much more doable. The team challenged us on our impact during the co-headship and there were some extremely difficult conversations and questions asked during the inspection but we were determined we were not going to give an inch and we came out fighting.

In reality, the very fact that there were two of us meant that we could almost take turns in the meetings with one revving up with more evidence or points to make whilst the other was talking. We joked together that we were a relentless tag team and celebrated together when, on the second day of the inspection, we were given the news that all aspects of the school were good and that the report would specifically mention that the co-headship was a strength of the school. I've cried twice at work before. Once was on the day I left Latimer after 13 years and the other was when we got that result. So unused to me showing any kind of extreme emotion (Claire often referred to me as 'iron knickers'), so rare was it for me to cry or hug or do anything other than laugh that when I lay my head down on my folded arms on the table and sobbed uncontrollably at the end of the meeting I think she thought I was genuinely ill. The fact was I was just so relieved (and also massively sleep-deprived thanks to my first insomniac child). I was so proud that we'd done it. We had proved to everyone that co-headship could work and the school, its staff, its community and its pupils had the result they deserved. Had the co-headship been the weak link which had let the school down I would have been devastated. As it was, it was a strength of the school and I've never been more proud at work than that day when Claire and I could say we'd done right by the school and hadn't let them down.

That experience taught us that we could do it. Between that and the next inspection, we grew in knowledge, experience and confidence. When the next inspector came to visit we were sure that not only was the co-headship working effectively but that we now had a longer track record of continuous improvement to share and we were proud of what the school was achieving in all areas. This second inspection wasn't exactly a spa day but, my goodness me, it was different. We still don't know if the inspector knew this at the time but we were both pregnant, Claire with her second and me with my third, as was our deputy and multiple other staff across the school. This might not have been relevant to anyone else but we were acutely aware that if the inspector twigged and had any doubts about the leadership of the school then we were nervous this might affect their judgement if they thought we'd both be going off (alongside a significant number of other staff) again fairly soon. What ensued between Claire and me was a bizarre collection of big scarves, floaty outfits, giant coats and lots of sitting down behind high tables or counters, as Claire describes it, 'like when an actress in a soap is pregnant but her character isn't so they have to keep hiding her behind things in scenes'.

We were probably doing the inspector's professionalism a massive disservice in that they might not have factored in our maternity leaves into their judgement but it is indicative of the high stakes nature of our accountability culture and associated structures (and the fact that we were desperate not to have our personal circumstances impact on the outcomes) that we went on with the pregnancy disguising farce. As it was, the inspector never mentioned the fact that almost every female in the school appeared to be pregnant and never made any reference or asked any questions of us as co-heads regarding our pregnancies so they were either the consummate professional or our frankly ridiculous soap star pregnancy tactics had concealed our bumps. As it was, the leadership of the school since the co-headship was established has never been judged as anything less than good. This goes to show that it doesn't matter if your co-headship has five babies in five years between it, it can still be done without a massive Inspector Gadget coat and professional discussions conducted from behind a half-closed door.

Part of me now wishes I could go back in time and talk with confidence about the extensive and detailed cover arrangements we had put in place and how these arrangements were not detrimental to the school but a chance for other school leaders to gain experience in a headship role. Instead of potentially weakening the leadership of the school, it was providing an opportunity for further upskilling the leadership team and offering real and impactful opportunities for staff development. I speak to many women who want to go into leadership but are made to feel that effective leadership, maternity and parenthood cannot coexist. I know the fact that we went through the concealment farce ourselves was indicative of a system which has this bias held by many, running very deeply throughout all layers of their beliefs, accountability mechanisms and attitudes. It saddens me now to look back and see the younger versions of Claire and myself who felt that was necessary. I would urge anyone who has any sway in leadership or education to work hard to ensure that no parent or pregnant woman ever feels under this same pressure, however light-hearted it seems. Pregnancy and parenthood should have no bearing on the ability of a leader to lead and the subsequent Ofsted judgements, pupil results, staff retention and overall development of the school are a testament to the fact it is possible. It is just so sad that so many people, including both those who are responsible for inspecting or appointing leaders, as well as aspirant and existing leaders themselves, still hold the belief that parenthood and leadership are not compatible. I have lost count of the number of times I have coached women who have contacted me with the question, 'I want to go for a leadership post but I also want to try for a family; what should I do?' It is an absolute outrage that scores of our talented female aspirant leaders feel somehow that it is an either/ or decision and it could be viewed as an interesting reflection of our education system, our wider society and our potential biases that I have also never been contacted by a male colleague asking the same question.

It makes me so happy to hear of other successful co-headships being set up. The model really does appear to be gathering pace in recent years and it is always a delight when a potential new co-head gets in touch to ask if I have any advice which I'm always happy to share. In fact, I've chatted through the following points with scores of co-leadership partnerships, including over a dozen sets of co-headships now, and I have a 100% strike rate with successful appointments to date so I'm hopeful that the information has been a useful addition during the application and interview process.

The first thing I always ask/tell any potential co-heads is to make sure you align on the big things. If you're aligned with these then the smaller things and day-to-day decisions are much easier. Interview processes for co-heads can take many forms, you may be interviewed separately, together or a mix of both so it makes sense to have spent time together beforehand to nail down what your values, vision, ethos and beliefs are. Once you've done this, which may take more than a single quick chat but would hopefully develop over some time and through a considered process, then looking at potential interview questions together and thinking how you might answer them is a good activity. This is not to try and 'get your stories straight' but to see how you could answer in a way which shows both your alignment but also your own unique skills, expertise and knowledge. You are not trying to 'be' each other but to present a partnership and a united front. A true partnership is not two clones of each other but a complementary and well-balanced blend.

Once you've identified each other's skills and knowledge you may want to spend some time looking at each aspect of the headteacher or leader role and thinking about how you will carve this up. If we assume (for ease of explanation) that you're in a 50/50 job-share, but if you're not you can take these principles and apply them to other proportions.

So, you can both be:

  a) 50% responsible for 100% of the stuff. This means that you both do a little bit of all the job

  OR

  b) 100% responsible for 50% of the stuff. This means you both have specific parts of the job for which you're responsible

  OR

  c) 100% responsible for 40% of the stuff and the remaining 20% are shared or joint aspects which can't be neatly carved up or delineated.

You may ask why you need to be so specific but it is hugely important when sharing a role that you are clear about who does what. This isn't just so you both don't end up duplicating stuff and wasting time but it's also important for clarity. Staff will know who to go to, who is line managing them, who is responsible for certain things in the school and who should be the recipient of emails or invited to meetings, etc. One thing we found early on in the co-headship was that the staff felt that they had to report everything to both of us which was only making more work for them. We had to very quickly communicate to them that if you had informed one of us then that was enough; we would make sure the other one was notified. This wasn't because of anything other than the staff settling into the new structure and wanting to do a really good job. We were very lucky that we had such a hardworking team and it was up to us to reassure them that, although we were two people, there only needed to be one message or report. This also meant that emails were interesting to manage. We had separate email accounts to which our individual teams would report but we also had a co-heads email which served as the official channel for whole school and community communication. One of us would man this account on our days in and then forward anything of importance to the individual email addresses. By keeping our teams separate we didn't become overwhelmed by extraneous or irrelevant information, but we also had a central store via the co-heads email for joint work.

Accountability is an important consideration not only for staff who are alongside co-leaders but for co-leaders themselves, which is why the aforementioned percentages are so important. We were fortunate in that during our co-headship neither of us had any issues with our performance but looking back this could have been rather naïve as it was potentially luck. People's performance can take a nosedive for any number of reasons. It may be a period of mental or physical ill-health, a bereavement, a new caring commitment, a relationship breakdown, a change in personal circumstances, or anything which may cause a dip in performance for anyone in any role. Leaders are human and human lives are messy, complicated and unpredictable and leaders are not immune to these. Without a clear outline of who is responsible for what then it can place a potentially unnecessary burden on one half of the leadership pair and, at worst, lump all performance together in an inaccurate homogenous mess if one half of the performance dips whilst the other half is working well and at capacity.

It has implications for performance managing the co-leadership role too. It would be immensely difficult for a performance manager to sift through the interwoven threads of who managed to achieve what in a co-leadership role unless there is a clear outline of which bucks stop where and with whom. Claire and I chose to carry out our performance management meetings together. We had a 'no secrets' way of working and again this may have been helped by the fact that we were also friends so knew most of the details of each other's home lives, which I appreciate not all would like to share in a co-leadership model. This meant that there was nothing which wasn't shared in the role. We were given individual targets relating to our own knowledge and skills development, as well as our individual teams, but we were also given some shared targets which we needed to work on together. I would advocate this as a really strong model. The inclusion of both individual and shared targets means that as individuals you can still show impact, progression and professional growth but you are also encouraged to work on things together. Claire and I shared nearly everything in the role and never needed encouragement to take on joint projects but, depending on the structure and nature of a co-leadership role and the individual personalities, I can see that ensuring there is a degree of joint accountability would help to cement the role as one role which is co-led rather than two separate individuals who have carved up a job of work. It is so important to work seamlessly as a twosome and to present that united front. If not, you risk looking like a badly coordinated pantomime horse which could, at any moment, split in the middle to reveal instead of a glorious partnership, simply a big head and a massive rear end.

To present that united front requires communication not just across the wider staff but between each other. What we learnt in co-headship was that communication genuinely moves from clunky and inefficient to slick and almost telepathic the longer you are in a co-leadership role. It is a little like those celebrities that go on Strictly Come Dancing who, in terms of grace and dancing skill, are initially not dissimilar to that pantomime horse but who, after weeks of training, can dazzle the audience and deal with any samba or quickstep which is thrown at them. I know we trialled all sorts of methods of communication – digital, handwritten, books, post-it notes, emails, whiteboards, texts, you name it we tried it. But the fact of the matter was that the longer we did the job, the better we got at it, the fewer 'new' things or problems we had to solve and so the fewer things we had to communicate to each other. We went from firefighting and every day being a new thing which we hadn't experienced before, thus needing to discuss it, to thinking, 'oh, this old chestnut again' and knowing exactly how to deal with it. It meant that there was a distinct shift from procedural and managerial communication to strategic and longer-term communication. Yes, we still needed to update each other but not for as long, in as much depth or with as much 'peer to peer counselling' which accompanied many of our early days as we got to grips with the role and its challenges.

Initially, we had six days of headship within the co-headship to allow for us to carry out the bulk of all leadership as we had not initially replaced our own deputy roles. This amount of crossover reduced as the co-headship developed to the point where we were rarely there together in the final part. We would still meet at governor meetings, other events and open days but gone was the need to have each other there for deliberate communication as our roles and experience developed. This is a model which I wish other co-leadership roles would explore, this sliding scale of crossover moving from a lot of crossover in the early days to a reduction going forward and as the co-leadership develops. It is an investment in the early days which reaps huge dividends later in terms of efficiencies and a flexible use of the co-leadership time itself which I'll explore in more detail later.

Claire and I were laughing recently about some of our early communication crossover attempts, some were beyond awful and in our defence our co-leadership role predated a lot of the more recent software which is designed for this kind of instant secure communication but our early attempts were pretty clunky. One thing which never failed though were those days where it was just us two, a big piece of sugar paper and a massive packet of felt tip pens (Claire was always scribe as my handwriting looks not dissimilar to if you'd dipped a drunk tarantula in ink and set it loose on the page). The conversations, debate, challenge, laughter and strategic thinking you can have over a big sheet of actual paper whilst both kneeling on the floor and peeling off multiple post-it notes should not be underestimated. Face-to-face conversation between the two of us and real, concrete joint planning was what worked and cemented many of the bones of both our small and grander plans. If you looked down the side of our filing cabinet you'd have seen loads of rolls of these sheets of paper and if you'd unrolled them it would have been like an archaeological dig through the development of the co-headship.

If co-leadership is to work then these face-to-face days are so important but these need to be alongside a real and shared understanding of the life and work of the school. So, alongside the communication of the legal or business or necessary stuff was the need to keep a running update of what was going well and what was brewing which maybe wasn't as savoury. It was as important to update each other with brilliant ideas colleagues had suggested or assemblies which had been uplifting and full of joy as it was about an ongoing rumbling parental complaint or the fact that a colleague's return to work meeting needed doing. We needed to update each other about the child who had done a great piece of work or who had scored for their team at the weekend. We needed to tell each other about the parent who'd just had the new baby or the fact that the harvest collection was looking massive just as much as we needed to discuss that there was a parent with a huge lunch money deficit who was contesting it.

These may sound like small things but these are the fabric of the life of the organisation. These are the things that involve the pupils and the families we serve and the staff who make up our school community. If we are not investing in communication about these aspects of our organisations then what are we communicating? If we are to live our ethos, straplines and vision statements then, yes, in leadership we need to communicate about budgets, spreadsheets and data drops. However, what makes a school or an organisation a truly brilliant place is when the most important things make up the bulk of the communication and, in a school, if you're not communicating information about people, be that your pupils, their families or their staff then what is the focus of your communication? It is a skill to know what information can and should be prioritised. In a school, it is information about children. Great teaching and leading is about effective relationships and moving forward together in a shared direction. How can you move anyone or anything if you don't know anything about your children or worse, don't regard that important?

As a leader, the moment we start to think it more important to know a child as a percentage on a spreadsheet rather than the fact that they just spoke publicly in assembly for the first time or have just started to stay at dad's new house at weekends then that's the time we need to revisit why we got into education in the first place. I appreciate that in larger organisations it can be a challenge to get this level of detailed knowledge about your pupils and staff but I would always argue that the more you know your children and your staff, the better decisions you will make for and with them, and the more likely it is that the vision you are trying to create will come to fruition. Some days, even though I was swamped with work, I'd often just go for a wander around the school and chat to kids or join in with whatever some were up to in lessons. Sometimes this was strategic, for example, if I felt I didn't know a year group well enough and sometimes it was because, quite frankly, I was bored or frustrated and needed to reconnect with what exactly we were trying to achieve and who we were doing it for.

So, you were just as likely to find me joining in with Year 3 PE as you were in my office or in rehearsals for the nativity as in a meeting. Within co-leadership where you may not be in as many days, this kind of time is even more precious. If the days you are in are already reduced then connecting with your students and staff and communicating with them and finding out about them should be something you try to work into every day for as much time as you can. If you are a part-time leader, the temptation can be to squeeze every minute of work out of your 'days in' and to schedule meeting after meeting, but it is so important to leave time to be present. Being out on the gate in the morning or afternoon, being in the dinner hall or on the playground or simply having a wander around the corridors and classrooms will yield far more useful and meaningful information as well as building trust, relationships and embedding you in the fabric of school life.

Presence while in a part-time role brings its challenges in terms of carving up who goes where and when. Governor meetings may fall on the same day every week and that may not be one of your agreed contracted days. For me, in many years of my co-headship, I attended almost all of them as I knew this was a better use of my time than trying to catch up on the information and not getting the opportunity to be part of the conversation. Claire and I only had one vote between us as co-heads to avoid cancelling each other out, but we'd always talk through the issues and decide on our stance. It's an important point to note for anyone setting up or part of a co-leadership role to consider voting on anything and how many votes a co-leadership position should have. Other events, such as parent open evenings, induction evenings, discos, fetes, evening performances, we shared as much as possible unless it was the kind of event where it was important we were both there such as the open evening for new starters in EYFS where we were meeting families for the first time. Most of the events would divvy up fairly equally depending on our responsibilities and teams in schools but it is an important aspect of maintaining the *entente cordiale* of a co-leadership position to decide and agree who is responsible for extra-curricular attendance.

One aspect of communication which we had inadvertently overlooked – as had our governors and pretty much everyone – was what we would do if we wanted to end the co-headship. There is much excitement at the moment about setting up co-leadership positions but in this first flush of love with the idea, there is little thought as to what might happen if one half of the partnership wants to call time on it. I won't lie, the decision to leave Latimer remains the hardest decision I've ever made. I loved and still love the bones of that place and I'm yet to find another school on all of my current edu-adventures which is even half as special as that one. However, my personal circumstances meant that there was no longer that neat alignment between work and home and I felt that I was going to have to step away from everything we'd worked so hard to set up and make a success. No one really talks about ending a co-leadership or any shared role. It is made all the more gut-wrenching because you are not only affecting your own life and making a big decision but you are affecting your work partner's too. I've never felt more sick, like more of a traitor or more awful than when I had to tell Claire. We'd worked so hard, laughed, cried, become parents together, shared anything and everything for years and now I was walking away. Thankfully, she is not only a consummate professional, one of the world's greatest and kindest humans but also a pragmatist. She knew that we had no exit plan and so contacted the governors for their thoughts.

In the spirit of the initial co-headship setup, it was the governors who championed a second new way of working. The result was a new leadership structure with Claire maintaining an 'executive head' role and the creation of a new 'head of school' role. Incidentally, it was the built-in staff development for our middle and senior leaders – provided through our associated maternities – which had allowed colleagues to step up into senior positions, facilitating a lot of this restructuring flexibility and making it so successful. It was fortunate that our governors were incredibly skilled and innovative, as well as recognising the ongoing benefits of retaining key staff through new and different ways of structuring roles. From worrying that the only option would be for

Claire to become full-time or appoint someone to replace me directly, our governors once again tore up the rulebook and created a new structure which continues to go from strength to strength, having had yet more successful Ofsted inspections and academic outcomes. Communication about exit strategies is something which we learnt should have been on the table from the beginning but when you're building a house, your initial thoughts aren't how you might demolish or repurpose it, it's just to get the damn thing built with a working kitchen and toilet that flushes.

My advice, therefore, to anyone setting up a co-leadership would be not only to think carefully about how to divvy up work, who is accountable for what and how you are going to communicate but also what you would do should one of you decide to leave or was unable to carry on in the current setup. Claire and I used to say we couldn't imagine working as we did in our type of co-headship with anyone else. Trusts, boards and employers need to think carefully about their co-leadership structures and analyse whether they set up the co-leadership based on personality or because they believed in the principles of and the benefits a co-leadership structure provides. This should not preclude a co-leadership model from being on the appointment table but appointers need to be clear about what they would do if one (or both) of the co-leaders wanted or needed to leave. Would they want to replace one half directly? Would they expect one half to go full-time? Would they explore a new potential structure? Just as the departure of a solo leader presents challenges and opportunities for innovation so too does the departure of a co-leader. Succession planning is one way to help replace a departing colleague but so are other options such as restructuring. Effective talent identification and management can go some way to providing a staff where there are colleagues ready and interested in taking on co-leadership but there also needs to be a backup plan to help steady the ship or chart a new course should things take an unexpected leadership turn. This can require more innovative thinking when dealing with an existing co-leadership post as any departure affects two people – the departee and the remaining staff member. The responsibilities and skills of the makeup of the co-leadership position could, therefore, somewhat dictate any proposed solutions.

What co-leadership does is (in my experience both as a co-leader and from talking to many settings and co-leaders across the sector) provide more benefits than it does challenges or barriers, which I'll talk more about later. Perhaps the greatest benefit is that it allows for innovation, balance, challenge and dispensing with a leadership hierarchy that only fits a very singular narrative or structure. Just like Run-DMC and Aerosmith produced something new and innovative, which many thought in principle could not or should not work, what it proved was that when two highly-skilled people or groups are brought together then the overall co-leadership whole is greater than the sum of its individual parts. With this in mind, if anyone is considering setting up a co-leadership position either as an employer or as a co-leader then I would always urge you to channel your inner Run-DMC and Aerosmith and encourage new thinking and ways of working and to encourage your aspirant leaders to 'Walk This Way'.

Questions to consider

Employers	Flexible workers
Are the senior team aware of the wider range of different co-leadership structures available? Have case studies been explored and flexi leadership models discussed in terms of benefits and challenges for the organisation?	Have you discussed alignment on the 'big issues' with a potential co-leadership partner? Have you audited and identified both of your skills, knowledge and experience to identify both what is your combined offer and what you both bring as individuals?
How many flexible leaders does the organisation have? How many would it like to develop? In which roles? In which part of the organisation?	Have you practised how you would answer interview questions or tasks to showcase your own talents as well as presenting a complementary blend as co-leaders?
Are there any local successful co-leadership roles which you could contact and discuss how the co-leadership works in a local context?	Have you connected with Flex Teach Talent or Shared Headship Network and explored their 'matching' tools and events as well as their case studies and guidance?
How many votes would a co-leadership model get in a decision-making process such as a governors' meeting?	How will you ensure clear lines of communication with staff about who does what in the co-leadership?
How would a co-leadership model be divided up? 50% of 100%, 100% of 50% or 100% of 40% and then a shared 20%. Has a skills analysis been done of the co-leaders and tasks/aspects allocated accordingly?	What will you both do if there is a problem within the co-leadership? How will you deal with conflict or disagreement?
Is there an exit strategy for the co-leadership role as well as a setup strategy?	How will you communicate with each other? What software, tech or meeting schedule will be used?
How will accountability and performance management work?	How will you assign extra-curricular events attendance?
Has line management of the wider staff been discussed and a plan shared with them how the co-leadership will work in a day to day context?	Do you have an agreement about contacting each other on your days off?
How will you ensure ongoing professional development for both co-leaders and avoid deskilling?	How will you proactively ensure you do not become deskilled?

Employers	Flexible workers
Are there succession plan opportunities or secondments which could benefit from a co-leadership model?	How would you prefer to conduct performance management meetings? Together? Separately?
What would be any objections to a co-leadership model in your organisation? How might you address or counter these? Why might the objections have arisen?	
Do you proactively encourage flexible working applications to leadership roles? How is this communicated in your advertising and recruitment materials?	
What communication or handover time could be built into the role? Is a sliding scale model possible?	

Track ten: Call Me

Blondie

Oh my word, I *love* Debbie Harry. She's one of the first-ever musical performances I ever remember seeing on TV when I was about three or four years old and it was love at first sight. I am word-perfect on pretty much all of Blondie's back catalogue and adored everything from her voice and her style to her music. But Blondie was the name of a group, not just a reference to Debbie Harry's hair colour. She co-founded the group with her guitarist boyfriend Chris Stein. In fact, so many people assumed that Blondie was just Debbie Harry that the group had a badge campaign which read, 'Blondie is a group'. I love that Blondie was co-founded by two members and that they smashed so many stereotypes and blended so many genres of music.

You see, partnerships so often yield so much more creativity and groundbreaking developments than one going solo, but in relation to flexible working, successful models are all too often attributed to being anomalies – the 'one-hit wonders' – rather than enduring models of effective partnership. I can think of so many wonderful, memorable or well-known musical partnerships spanning many decades and genres from Dean Martin and Frank Sinatra, through to Simon and Garfunkel, Marvin Gaye and Tammi Terrell, DJ Jazzy Jeff and the Fresh Prince and onto other partnerships such as the Pet Shop Boys, Wham! and then Little Mix and Stormzy. The list and genre types are seemingly endless once you start thinking about them and this is something we should bear in mind when thinking about job-sharing. We spoke in the co-leadership chapter about the idea of the sum of the parts being greater than the whole and I believe this is so true in job-sharing.

As we've already touched on, two people bring a range of skills, knowledge and experience, both professional and lived, and they may be very different people too which gives twice the opportunity for children to relate or connect with their educator. I know from my own children's experience in school and 22 years in primary that children, like adults, just seem to gel better with some teachers than others and often there is no rhyme or reason to this. It's just individual personalities rather than a reflection of the teacher's skill, knowledge or expertise. I am not going to paint a rosy picture though. Job-sharing requires a particular mindset and way of working for it to be truly effective and believe me when I say I have seen some pretty disastrous job-shares across the many schools in which I've worked in and supported.

The first element is relationship. Before a job-share can even get off the ground there is no point setting it up if the two job-sharers are sworn enemies or can't stand each other. I have seen both two very different people and two very similar people make brilliant job-shares but I have also seen the converse for both setups. Both sides of a job-share do need to get on before agreeing to the job-share. It's easy to swerve someone you don't really like if you don't work too closely with them; it's easy then to keep things professional, light and polite but not engage with them too much if they're the kind of person who makes your teeth itch. This is much harder if you have to work in very close proximity and communicate effectively and regularly which you do in a job-share. You obviously don't need to be best pals with your job-share but you do need to have a relationship where you are not trying to resist screaming, rolling your eyes or tearing your hair out every time they enter the room. We need to ensure that there is enough emotional, professional and relationship capital there to set up an effective working partnership.

This is a really important consideration not only for job-sharers but also for those who are in charge of setting up or organising appointments for job-shares. Thinking rather idealistically that because everyone is a professional then there should just be an automatic assumption that everyone can simply get on with a job of work and put any personal feelings aside is a little naïve. It's possible but, my goodness me, it's draining.

Ever been in a meeting with someone who you are finding utterly infuriating? Ever tried to argue your point with someone who resolutely refuses to budge on their point of view? Ever worked with anyone who categorically refuses to pull their weight or who deliberately appears to be misunderstanding everything you say? I'm sure it's more than possible to keep your cool and remain professional for the duration of whatever meeting or session that was but I bet you had an internal mental rant to yourself or maybe to your partner that night or a confidential conversation with a trusted colleague/ mentor about your frustrations and to gain their perspectives and help you evaluate why things panned out like they did. Now imagine having to share your entire role with that person, every aspect of your job. Imagine having to plan, communicate and talk directly to them every day and be jointly accountable for the relative success of the role. It's doable but that's not a healthy setup and will gradually wear down both sides of the job-share until it is a very toxic situation or one person feels completely demotivated and their confidence is shattered. I have seen it many times at all levels of responsibility across many organisations.

This is not to say that job-sharing has to be done by two people who are absolute bosom buddies who are able to telepathically connect and always work seamlessly without even a hint of friction or discontent. That too would be pretty far from reality. What we need for effective job-shares is a recognition that we are asking two individual people to blend their approaches and their practice to provide a complementary set of skills and knowledge and to set up a mutually supportive structure within which they can work. With the best will and professionalism in the world, not all partnerships or pairings will be able to work like this and so, just as we are looking at the make up of our teams when appointing a new single appointment and think how they would fit into the existing team, so too do we need to pay attention to this when setting up a job-share.

We can't simply say that Miss X wants to work 0.6 and Mr Y needs to teach 0.4 alongside his other duties in school so they can just go together. It is more than fitting pegs in holes and piecing together of a staffing puzzle, it is a weaving together of skills and the building of successful partnerships which are mutually supportive and ultimately which are of greatest benefit to our students. There will be no benefit to our students if, driven to utter distraction, an externally equanimous Miss X is potentially spending a disproportionate amount of their joint PPA time actually fantasising about Mr Y's untimely demise whilst he's banging on about something as she can't see how she can possibly spend one more minute working with him. I recognise that is an extreme and somewhat exaggerated and flippant description of a scenario but I have seen first hand in multiple schools how some job-shares have gradually eroded the energy, confidence and will to stay in the profession simply due to a personality clash. I have also seen how those same professionals, when in a different partnership, have flourished and thrived. Therefore, when setting up a job-share, care needs to be taken to do much more than a simple timetable analysis but also to do some form of skills, expertise and amiability analysis. Ensuring partnerships are effective will also help with retention and ultimately therefore staffing continuity.

Once an effective working partnership is identified then communication is key. Just as I have outlined in the co-leadership chapter, communication between job-sharers is crucial. Every partnership will be unique so every partnership will ultimately find its own way of working that fits best with their working patterns but there are a few basic principles to consider for both employers of job-sharers and the job-share partners themselves.

Like in the co-leadership considerations, there need to be clear lines of accountability and clearly defined roles and responsibilities. When things are going well it is easy to identify the specific achievements of each individual within the job-share and tailor any professional learning, but equally it is important to have clear areas of accountability if one person within the job-share is either underperforming, temporarily unable to continue with their role or if they leave permanently mid-year. Having clear accountability outcomes is protection for the other job-share who may initially be very stretched, wrong-footed or feel somehow responsible if there are significant changes to the effectiveness or make up of the job-share. Although it is two people carrying out one role, it is important to retain and protect the view of each as an individual when addressing issues around performance and effectiveness. There is also much that the employer can do to facilitate effective communication such as ensuring joint PPA time or providing some additional release time for handover or joint planning and moderation. Although many job-share partnerships find a rhythm as to what works for them for much of the day-to-day business, the onus on developing effective communication and joint work opportunities should not lie solely with the job-sharers, especially if one or both end up working significant additional hours for which they are not paid. As with the model outlined in the co-headship chapter, these communication or handover periods often become much slicker as a job-share develops so an initial investment in the early days may not continue to be necessary as the job-share becomes more established.

Care should also be taken when scheduling training, meetings and other whole staff or department events. It is important to have an overview of as much of the academic year as possible and to identify which staff definitely need to attend which elements of meetings and training and on which dates and then to communicate this as early as possible. The reason so many people will already be working in a job-share set up is to balance additional commitments outside the workplace; last-minute urgent meetings or training events can be incredibly stressful for the part-time worker as they feel the weight of the need to attend; the professional interest and want to progress and develop; the not wanting to miss out or be on the back foot; and then balancing these against what might already be a very finely balanced childcare or other caring responsibility or duty. Until I had children myself (and then with each subsequent one I had) I did not fully understand the military precision with which each working day had to be planned in order to ensure that each of the children was picked up, dropped off, ferried to and fed at the correct times. I lived in fear of one of their childcare arrangements falling through, meetings over running or being the last parent to collect from their setting. If I had to work on a day I usually didn't, and at short notice, it was unbelievably difficult as my husband usually works away in the week; my nursery had to have additional days booked weeks in advance and grandparents were often either unable to fit three car seats in their car to do the pick ups or were working themselves.

It should never be underestimated just how finely balanced so many of our colleagues' lives are and not just those with small children. So many of our colleagues have huge commitments outside the role (not just our job-sharers and flexi workers) and it is more than courtesy to give as much notice as we can for meetings and changes; it is imperative for their overall wellbeing and the feeling that they are in control and not having additional pressure put upon them. It is also a practice that can actively preclude a truly representative and diverse staff and leadership body from developing. If the only staff able to attend additional training or other opportunities at short notice are those who are in good health, who have no caring commitments or dependants and have the wealth and flexibility of time to switch up their diaries at the drop of a hat then we are slamming the developmental door in a lot of faces. If we again look at the demographic of who tends to work flexibly in education (according to the Department for Education statistics), it is women; this is the same demographic which is the one most likely to leave education after retirees. Now I know that teaching, especially primary teaching, is dominated by women but that does not mean that we should accept the status quo of flexible workers, who almost make up the largest number of flexible workers, being the ones most likely to miss out on training and development opportunities due to their flexible working setup.

Just like with opportunities for pay progression, no worker should feel that they are under pressure to attend training or meetings for which they are not paid or to feel huge unnecessary additional stress or pressure because of last minute changes that could be avoided. It is also downright unfair and wrong to suggest a part-time worker attend 100% of meetings or training in line with full-time staff. If those meetings cannot be accommodated in that worker's normal contracted hours and their associated pro rata meeting and INSET attendance then they should be paid for their attendance, otherwise they are potentially the only person in the room not being paid to be there. Add in the additional costs of commuting, potential extra childcare and so on and many would actually be *paying* to be there. It is a situation I have found myself in many times. I have been asked to speak at an event to school leaders or other groups so not only will I be being asked to prepare materials, arrange childcare, incur additional travel costs and any other associated expenses (as well as losing time out of my already very finely balanced work/home commitments) then I have found myself being expected to do this for no payment. Now I am not an educator who would expect more than my usual rate of pay from my day job (plus whatever any significant costs were to get me there if it was outside my usual region) but on occasions when I have asked if there is any payment associated with the speaking I have been told 'no' and the person has actually been very surprised that I have asked the question. This is indicative of a system that has a 'full-time work' default mindset and structure. Others in attendance as delegates at the event where I've been asked to speak will generally all still be in receipt of a full-time wage despite being out of school or their organisation. As a part-time worker who is being asked to come in during the working week in addition to my part-time contract, I am technically expected to just come along and speak for no payment (or actually incur a cost).

Now I have mentioned my brilliant line manager, our deputy CEO, before. He is fabulous at managing my diary and working out what I do and don't have to go to, and ensuring that if it is in addition to my usual role, then I will get paid. Believe me (and I speak from multiple experiences), there is nothing more frustrating than standing up in front of a roomful of people who are on full-time (and sometimes very large) salaries and delivering the training only to realise that you're the only one in the room not actually being paid. So brilliant and vigilant are my employers though that if there is training they feel is necessary for me to attend on a day in addition to my contracted time, not only can I attend the training but I'll also get paid. You might think that it's odd I say that's brilliant, as surely that's what all employers should do, but I know from conversations where people have repeatedly been surprised when they've asked me to come and speak and I've asked if they can cover my normal leadership day rate and they've just said a flat no that they are actually an exception. I've also spoken to so many part-time colleagues from across the sector and the country on training courses who have said they are there on their 'day off' and have revealed their frustration at not being either paid or given time off in lieu. Being given time in lieu is what I did in my previous co-head role and also do now within my current role.

Everyone knows education is chronically underfunded but to expect part-time workers to work additional days without appropriate remuneration is simply wrong; it is at best an unintentional oversight by employers who may simply not be aware of all the decisions in school and at worst a deliberate money saving exercise by some pretty unscrupulous employers who are capitalising on that vulnerable feeling of the 'golden handcuffs'. It takes a very confident employee, especially if they are relatively junior, to raise the question with senior team members around additional payment in a time of ever dwindling funding, especially one that may already be feeling that golden handcuff debt of gratitude. It is, therefore, so important for line managers and leaders to be aware again about who their part-time workers are and being truly proactive like my line manager in ensuring that diaries are fair and pay packets are appropriate.

It is this kind of careful, deliberate and fair management and associated remuneration that truly breeds commitment, loyalty and trust and also why I know it can be done, as my CEO and deputy CEO have done with me over the last three years. Sadly this proactive diary monitoring and strategic thought about the commitments and payment associated with additional work for part-time workers that my line managers have done so well is not yet evident across the sector. Too many flexible and part-time workers are being asked to undertake significant amounts of extra work, training or other commitments without being paid.

Yes it's a headache to schedule diaries well in advance and yes it will impact on budgets to pay for additional days and training, but our workforce is our greatest asset as well as our biggest expenditure and to expect some to not be paid fairly for work should be resigned to the history books and actively called out by leaders, employees, trusts and boards. Those line-managing part-time workers do need to have diary management on their agendas when thinking about part-time colleagues. Regular review of diary commitments and a reshuffle of which meetings or events can be removed or rescheduled can play such a huge part in supporting part-time colleagues as well as demonstrating that they are a valued member of the team, not such an inconvenience that they should accept being underpaid. It is interesting when I think back again to Laura McInerney's speech I heard all those years ago about part-time teachers not doing a full-time job for a part-time wage. This doesn't just equate to planning, marking, reports and assessment but also to all aspects of the wider school and professional life.

Regular check ins for part-time staff go such a long way to making the part-time member of staff feel on a par with the full-time members of the wider teams. Scheduled regular meetings to catch up with information, review diaries and update with any changes or developments will never be time wasted. In my current role, my line manager will often schedule these electronically via my online diary or he'll just send me a quick message to say there have been a lot of developments in the last couple of days or weeks and have I got 20 minutes to have a chat. This serves so many purposes. As it is one-on-one then I don't feel 'stupid' for not knowing whereas in a larger meeting I might do. I get to ask questions and really understand what has gone on. It is a sign that my role and my impact is valued. Scheduling a one-on-one in our packed professional roles and then actually sticking to it and taking focused time with it communicates that that person is valued and matters. It also builds a really good relationship and link between the part-time worker and the organisation. Having the same person do the update meetings means that again you begin to get much slicker at communication and they then tend to need to be shorter and less frequent. By scheduling them in a proper meeting room or a scheduled online call, it also allows for no interruption or distraction that, again, sends a very clear message about being valued and also means that the meeting is crisp, focused and stays on track. Bringing both our diaries, our schedules and overviews of current projects to these meetings means that very quickly we can see exactly how projects are going and what next steps are.

These are not formal review meetings and neither are they scheduled weekly or even necessarily monthly. My line manager sets up a rolling calendar invite that we either keep or cancel depending on what we need. They remind me a little of the end of shift handover on a ward where one team updates the other with all that has happened and any future care plans. These meetings may be very brief and only a matter of minutes or they may be an hour or so but what they do is make a part-time worker feel very much connected to the organisation and very clear about the wider work, current focus and direction as well as a chance to have the kind of ad hoc conversation which as a part-time employee you don't get as many opportunities within the working day to have. This means that, when I am in work, I'm not spending half my life being surprised by things or trying to find out information. This simple investment in a short meeting means that the wheels are oiled and more of my time in my role is spent on my job of work rather than on information gathering. For any part-time worker or job-share, I would wholeheartedly encourage line managers to set up these regular short meetings. The time they take to carry out is miniscule in relation to the benefits they reap in terms of staff wellbeing, efficiency and focus.

We have mentioned a little about attending training and the importance of remuneration but another aspect which employee and employer needs to be vigilant about is potential deskilling. I know in our co-head role that Claire and I had very specific aspects with which we dealt and, if I had stayed in the role longer, I know that I would have needed further training in some areas or would have had to ask Claire to rotate some of our roles as there were huge sections of the role with which I was having little or no direct daily experience. Deskilling is a very easy and almost unnoticeable process that has real potential to take root in a job-share, especially an established one. Unless there is a real and concerted effort to rotate responsibilities, one half of the job-share can end up never teaching an aspect of the curriculum or never taking on a specific part of the role. This can often occur when one half of the job-share is particularly skilled at that aspect and so the job-share 'plays to its strengths' when carving up the role. This is great for student outcomes as they get the strongest educator in their favoured position but what it inadvertently does is potentially deskill the other half of the job-share who is not responsible for that area. There may be a degree of cross-pollination of skills just by the nature of two professionals planning, talking and delivering within the same role but, unless there is a deliberate and strategic ongoing development in all areas for both sides of the job-share, there may end up being a situation where one ends up being the star of a particular area, like Blondie, while the other one is almost forgotten.

It would be foolish to let a situation like this take hold as we have already discussed how people's lives are messy and nothing is forever. If the job-share ends or develops then having only one half of it that can do a particular aspect of the job is a rather precarious position. Deskilling is a real and present issue around job-sharing and, again, both the job-sharers and their employees need to be mindful of this and ensure that any professional learning development opportunities develop each professional's skills, not just the aspects of the role for which they are currently responsible. If they don't practise and develop these then, if they are required to go 'solo' again, they will potentially find this very challenging. It is also good sense to keep all of our employees development well balanced as the needs of the school will continue to change and if we are to have an agile and responsive workforce then we don't want to end up in the situation where we have accidentally allowed some of our staff to become deskilled. Setting up a job-share, therefore, requires strategy and review at all stages from its planning, inception, through its ongoing work and then (like in the co-leadership model discussed in previous chapters) have a clear plan for if one or both of the job-sharers want to alter their working pattern or leave.

Job-sharing can provide enormous balance, breadth, accessibility and improved retention within the individual organisation and the profession but it is a model that needs careful cultivation. It cannot simply be a 'blind date' approach of hurling two employees together and hoping for the best. Strategic, deliberate and ongoing review of the systems associated with supporting, and the ongoing review of a job-share's effectiveness and professional development needs should be part of any job-share setup. If we are to ensure that our job-shares are effective and not need the 'we are a group' badge campaign which Blondie needed in order to communicate their musical working structure then we need to be champions and advocates for not only the provision of the job-share structure itself but also a commitment to ensuring that both members of the job-share group are recognised and supported equally.

Questions to consider

Employers	Flexible workers
Are there clear accountability structures and mechanisms for job-shares?	Are you clear about who is responsible for what within your job-share?
Have extra curricular, meetings and training demands been considered when factoring in a job-share?	Have you clearly communicated your availability times for those days on which you are contracted to work and those on which you aren't?
Has consideration been given to any potential personality clashes within job-shares? What are the dynamics of your job-shares in terms of experience, approach, working practices, complementary skills and knowledge?	Are you aware of who to go to for support if the job-share is not working effectively?
What are the career development opportunities for your job-sharers? Is job-sharing modelled and available at all levels within your organisation?	Am I clear about how to claim for additional payment/overtime for any work outside my usual contracted hours? Am I proactive about keeping records of hours worked and flagging up that I am completing additional work?
Are job-sharers aware of how to tackle any problems or where they can go for support if they feel a job-share arrangement is not working effectively?	If I am in a job-share, how can I proactively ensure that I do not become deskilled? Can we rotate some elements of the job? Am I still ensuring I develop a full suite of skills and knowledge? What additional support or training might I need? Do I know who I need to approach with this?
How much of the additional tasks associated with a role are job-sharers being asked to do? Are colleagues on a 0.5 contract being expected to do the same as 0.8 or full-time? How can we ensure appropriate adjustments, remuneration or lieu time? Are requirements in a shared role proportionate to contracted hours?	
Are there clear plans for what to do in the event of a job-share needing to end? Is there a clear exit strategy to safeguard the other employee?	

Employers	Flexible workers
How are part-time colleagues contacted and have expectations about response times or mechanisms been discussed. Are all staff aware of communication protocols? How do you know?	
Are part-time workers brought up to speed in a timely and efficient fashion with information from their non-working days? What systems do you have in place for this? Are there opportunities for colleagues to speak about their experience of communication as a part-time or flexible worker?	

Track eleven: 22
Taylor Swift

If you ever go on a long car journey with me it is inevitable at some point that I will turn it into some kind of car disco and begin blasting out everything from Motown and '90s indie to northern soul and some sugary pop. Believe me, it's painful to hear, but every performance is exuberant and joyful, just maybe not enjoyable to the wincing captives in my car. One of my favourite singers to belt out at top volume is Taylor Swift. I've yet to hear a song of hers that doesn't end up as a complete ear worm and frankly my performance of her 'Love Story', complete with melodramatic actions, air grabs and closed eyes is worthy of an Oscar (or perhaps more accurately, a polite hand over my mouth). She's on most of my gym and running playlists and even featured on a leaving CD which Claire made for me when I left the co-headship (yes, we had a mix tape).

I'm pretty far from 22, but I regularly try to kid myself I could get away with 35 if the lighting was decent enough – shame I'm yet to find a decent enough light! Nonetheless, there's something about this song which makes me feel as if I could take on the world and do something completely new and unexpected, which if you know me there's a good chance I probably will. I have the attention span of a gnat, no 'idiot' filter between my brain and my mouth, don't mind making myself look like a bit of a twit, unbelievably clumsy and the number of people who say, 'I can't believe you just said/did that...' is ever growing. I'm not someone who is deliberately rude, offensive or who loves to invite conflict, quite the opposite. What I do though is constantly ask 'why' and – like my parents who I've mentioned have always done things differently – I'm not afraid to challenge the status quo or to ask what may be perceived as the 'stupid question'. I'm not one of those people who has a huge ego or is trying to be the cleverest or coolest in the room (I'm pretty far from that); I am genuinely inquisitive, love people but I am unafraid to just have a try at something or make myself look a bit silly if it means I get to truly understand something or help someone else. Listening to 22 makes me smile as it's simply *fun*. Fun and adventure are often under utilised or never thought of when exploring workforce reform and flexible working.

Occasionally we can be so bogged down in the day-to-day busyness and the ingrained historical structures and narratives that there can be no space for innovation or creativity. In the best organisations, time is carved out and diaries kept with deliberate gaps to enable not just the ploughing through of to-do lists but the cultivation of new ideas. My current role is not only one which I've hardly seen anywhere else, but it's also part-time and very flexible. That's three pretty unique elements to a role and it means, like Taylor Swift, that I'm solo most of the time. For flexible workers who are the only one in their organisation doing their job, especially a newly created or unique role there can be a unique set of challenges.

When I tried to explain my job to my mum I found it really tricky as there is no existing understanding or explanation for my role. She summed it up when she said, 'It was much easier when you were a head; I knew what that was!', and I often get asked, not just from my mum, 'Tell me again what it is that you do'. This doesn't bother me; in fact I just like to say, 'I work in education' to leave the whole thing open to interpretation. Funny thing is that most people don't question much after that so I'm not party to any misconceptions or preconceptions. It gives me quite a unique perspective too as, because not many people understand my role, it is fascinating how they then go on to frame what they say and talk about. It seems that job titles not only box in people in terms of roles but also in hierarchies relating to conversations. It's one thing I really love about Saturday CPD too. I remember meeting the two writers of my foreword Jonny and Sam at Kat Howard's book launch that was held in a function room above a popular local bar. When I was introduced I had no idea who they were (sorry!) and so I found myself chatting about all sorts. It was only when Jonny stood up to speak that I realised he was the CEO of a large trust and, after mentally scrolling back through everything I'd said so far that day with my 'Turner idiotic comment detector', I realised how brilliant it was that our conversations had been unencumbered by the social niceties and hierarchies which may have been present had we both been stood suited and booted at a corporate event with a neat little badge pinned to our jackets detailing our names and our roles. There is so much bound up in our small number of traditional job titles and to have such a narrow range of professional avenue options is surely limiting for our talented professionals as they move through their careers and are sifted and sorted into the traditional educational career boxes. Thankfully, there are the quiet rumblings of change beginning in many trusts and authorities and more unique roles are being created to develop and nurture the wide-ranging skills and talents within our diverse profession.

In a unique role there are ultimately unique challenges. For me, when I look back, my current work now bears little resemblance to the original job for which I applied. This is indicative of an organisation who don't pigeonhole or insist on specific traditional approaches but who champion innovation, individuality and nurturing professional interest and skills, as well as recognising that – just like the classes we teach – in education no two years are the same and so we need to be agile, well informed and responsive. Although some elements of my role remain the same (my involvement with early career teachers, my working with our trust's headteachers to share research and findings from reading and networks) the remainder of my role has morphed and shifted according to the needs of the trust and the wider profession. This has meant that I am constantly learning and developing which is hugely exciting and engaging.

Solo work is not all '22'-style fun and games, I'm sorry to tell you. It has the potential to be lonely, riddled with self-doubt and you might find yourself unsure as to whether you're doing a good job. The shared understanding of the work involved and what makes a successful educator in traditional roles, such as 'headteacher, teacher, deputy head, teaching assistant', mean that there are generally well understood and widely held beliefs about what constitutes a job well done. There are also established networks for aspirant leaders, Year 3 teachers, NQTs, headteachers, you name it and there's a support group or network to share ideas and provide guidance. However, when you're out there on your own doing your own thing in potentially your own way then there are none of these and this can be a wobbly place in which to be.

In my current role I had some of the confidence gleaned from the setting up of the co-headship and the associated 'navigating of newness' to steady my nerves and reassure me, but I won't lie and say that those early days weren't a little daunting. I felt the weight of all eyes on me as people welcomed me but asked, 'so what is it that you do?' You see, you can't really answer with, '*erm*, I'm not sure yet.' So I had to have a plan and fast. The original job description was a great place to start and then remembering that whatever I did needed to ultimately impact on outcomes for pupils served as my second guiding point. My seniors did a great job of giving just enough guidance and regular scheduled things to do (such as running the NQT training for them which I'd done for many years) to give me confidence but with just enough *carte blanche* for me to go away and develop everything else. One of the first and most useful things my line manager did was sit me down and talk me through the structure of the wider organisation across the trust and teaching school alliance. I was lucky in that I already knew quite a few people but having their exact roles explained and what they were responsible for made it absolutely clear who was doing what and so avoided crossover, duplication or accidental stepping on toes. I remember him reverting to my favourite method of communication (remember the big piece of paper and the felt tip?) and I kept that folded and taped into the front of my notebook for the entire first year and used to add to it every time I met someone new or spoke to someone on the phone.

This overview of who's who is so important when you're a solo flexer. You don't necessarily belong to any one team and so you don't necessarily automatically know what everyone does or have your own 'gang'. Getting up to speed with what everyone did and understanding their roles was a key part of my first few weeks. It would have been easy to just sit behind a laptop and type away but, just as getting to know a new class is the foundation of great teaching and learning, I wasn't going to get anywhere if I didn't know who was who. This didn't prevent me from making myself look like an absolute fool on occasions. I remember after the first few weeks wondering who on earth a lady (let's call her 'Sue') was who kept emailing me stuff. After about the 20th email I asked in the office (where I'd been chatting and happily working alongside them all for a while), 'Does anyone know who this Sue is who keeps emailing me; she's sending me all kinds of stuff and I've no idea who she is!' A lady, who was one of our senior staff members that worked only a couple of desks away, looked up bemused and said, 'It's me!' I'd somehow misheard her name and been labouring under the misapprehension for weeks that she was called (let's say) Sam. I still cringe about that now. Forging effective working relationships as a solo flexer is something which really does need work and I'm fairly sure most people aren't likely to endure quite the dozy Sue/Sam name debacle as me but we do need to recognise the potential for that feeling of being out of the loop which a solo flexer can feel.

As I have mentioned in previous chapters, lone workers are vulnerable. Being a lone worker, in a flexible part-time role makes you even more vulnerable as you can feel like you don't really belong anywhere. This is where organisational culture is so important. From day one, I never felt like I was an outsider. Yes, sometimes I felt a bit out of the loop or late to the party, but never enough that it has become an issue. I have always been made to feel that my work and ideas are valued, important and necessary and every team member – in our central team or out in our schools – has never been anything more than welcoming and gone out of their way to make me feel part of something bigger. This can be as simple as the wonderful headteacher, Halil Tamgumus, coming in to have a chat pre and post-session to check everything is OK. He's obviously a very busy professional but always makes the time to check in, see how I am and to comment on something positive. It is five minutes out of his day but the impact of that is that, despite having 'no fixed abode' as I work across our trust, I feel part of somewhere and something. It's also other examples such as one of our central team who will send me a message on social media or text to ask me not about work but about how I'm doing, to comment on the football scores or to ask me how my kids are doing. It was also in things like when we went on a leadership residential, one of the teams from our central office asking me if I wanted to join them all for a drink before dinner. These could seem like small courtesies but are all too often forgotten in people's busy lives and when you're a solo worker it would be easy to be accidentally left out or forgotten. It is indicative of a supportive culture when staff, in all teams and all locations, are overwhelmingly happy to see you, generous with their time and proactive in involving you.

As with any part-time role, communication within solo flexing is so important. Not only is there no one doing your exact role who might think, 'Oh, I must remember to tell Emma this as this is useful to our role' but there is no one who will be listening to any information with the same filter as you. You could argue that as every individual is unique then everyone listens with a unique filter but it's much more likely to have people listening with broadly the same important information filter if they are in the same or very similar roles. This is where lockdown has actually been hugely useful. The recording of multiple meetings has given me the opportunity to listen back to many meetings at different times which work for me and to listen with my own filter on, rather than having to rely on anyone else to note the salient points for me. My line managers are excellent at signposting opportunities for development or relevant emails and ensuring these land with me but no one will be in the middle of the same piece of thinking or research as me and, therefore, will not necessarily make the connections I would. Recorded meetings are hugely useful for solo flexi workers as they allow huge swathes of information to be accessed by us directly and not relayed by a third party who has a different filter.

Developing presence is also an important part of solo flexing. It is not about being a brash, loud and unforgettable for the wrong reasons but recognising that attention does need to be paid to establishing a presence in your absence. Now I suppose you could go down the route of a cardboard cut out of yourself placed somewhere strategically to enable you to remain in everyone's consciousness but I doubt this is a particularly safe or effective strategy. One thing that really worked for me was when I first joined the role, it was suggested that I join Twitter. This meant I could follow and comment on our schools' and colleagues' accounts and so not only remain informed about the wider work of the trust, which was really useful for my role, but also meant that I could comment and retweet and remain part of the organisation in my absence. So although I may not have interacted with colleagues face-to-face for a period, I had maintained that connection via social media. The schools and colleagues following my profile also meant that they were finding out what I did during times when I was not working directly with them so the flow of information was two way. Use of other messaging software such as Microsoft Teams also means that I am party to information which can be picked up on days when I'm not in a particular office or school. I'll admit that I hated Teams at first but have gradually fallen grudgingly into reluctant love with it, especially during lockdown as a means to keeping in touch with colleagues. Teams allows for a much more personable element as a quick teams video call lets you see your colleagues whereas an email can often feel impersonal when you have little face-to-face contact with a colleague.

I have outlined in previous chapters the importance of KIT and review meetings for job-sharers and these are even more important for solo flexers. The flexible nature of my role, both in terms of work type and working hours, means that these meetings are really important both in terms of how I am contributing to the strategic development of the organisation as well as keeping my diary manageable, my work targeted and my professional skills and knowledge up to date.

What solo flex provides is flexibility not only for the employee but for the employer. When additional leadership projects have come into the trust and there is no capacity for full-time staff to take on any more, I am frequently asked if I would like to take on a project. This built-in 'leadership reserve' or 'skills reserve' is an often overlooked aspect of flexible working. Just like a football squad there will be players who play full games, players who play parts of a game and that flexibility to bring players on and off would not be possible without capacity in the staff squad. By having me 'on the bench' I am able to pick up additional work or support the wider work of the team. A team who has no subs bench and only 11 players playing full-time is actually quite vulnerable as if one of their players has to leave the field then the remaining ten have to work much harder to share the load of the game. That is not to say that flexible workers are somehow only substitutes for full-time workers. Just as a football squad may field different teams in different ways depending on the fixture, so too can flexible workers ensure that an organisational squad has more than one way of fielding its teams and organising them to best effect. It also means that the flexible worker is able to develop their own skills not only within their initial or primary role but is able to use these in a broader range of contexts, thus negating some of the potential 'deskilling' that we discussed earlier.

Setting up a new solo flex role does require some degree of trust though, both from the employer and employee. A newly created or solo role doesn't necessarily have a blueprint for performance management or what simply constitutes a job well done. There is a degree of 'suck it and see' and an acceptance that there will undoubtedly be flux, changes of direction and alignment, some projects consigned to 'file 13' (AKA the bin), errors, learning points, flashes of brilliance, dead ends and eventually a shared understanding of exactly what the potential, strategy and impact of the role will be. This trust from both sides can only happen in a culture of openness and honesty. I remember the bewilderment of some of my early days where I was getting to know not only the staff but the structure and organisation of my new role, as well as trying to work out how I could be of most use to the trust and its wider networks.

During this period I had the security blanket of my usual familiar courses and collaboratives to run and I would advocate that at least some of any new role has absolute clarity around it in order to root the role in the day-to-day life of the organisation as well as to give structure and some degree of reassurance to the flexi employee. It was the wriggle room around these familiar territories though which proved to be most exciting. I could have potentially gone in any direction with my additional time but I chose instead to look not only to what the trust and local networks needed but to also look to national and international trends. I immersed myself in every book, blog, article, podcast and seminar I could find. It was a veritable smorgasbord of information and gradually I began to see how I could distil everything I had discovered into a workable strategy for my employers.

Now if I had been micro managed at this point, if I had every single working moment of my day allocated and accounted for then none of what subsequently happened would have happened. The very nature of a flexible role, especially a lone or newly created role means that there is space for further innovation and new ways of working. It is this 'hands off' approach in which creativity can thrive that can then permeate throughout the organisation. It can be daunting to not have every waking moment of your working life dictated, especially if you are used to working in a traditional role where you are super busy with zero time to review, evaluate or think of different things. So what did I do to avoid the potential overwhelm of this hands off, *carte blanche* approach? I revisited my old friends the giant sheets of sugar paper and felt tips. I nipped out of the office after a few weeks and sat in the large open corridor on the floor with dozens of books, papers and articles and a multitude of felt tip pens. I began to map everything I had discovered through my initial immersion in the role and found that everything fell rather neatly under five main areas. As I finished, by chance, my CEO and deputy CEO were coming down the corridor and stopped to see what I was doing. What resulted was to form the next two years of my role. Those five areas became threads within which I'd either work directly or support others to lead in. The big original piece of sugar paper is still rolled up in the back of my car, covered in scribble and post-it notes but that roll has become my role. The corridor conversation became a meeting with the senior team which became a series of headteacher meetings and training which became a new collaborative project across the trust which informed our initial teacher training and our early career support and is now part of the fabric of the work across the trust and beyond. Would that have happened if I had every aspect of my role mapped out? Unlikely.

Every new role in an organisation requires trust – trust that the employee will work hard and to the best of their abilities but also trust that whilst they develop and mould that new role, they will be supported by their employers. With the opportunities for relationship building, establishing a profile and the confidence from the day to day delivery and directed aspects of my role I was free to explore the possibilities of what the remainder of the role could become. This kind of adventuring into new lands and previously uncharted workforce models requires bravery, tenacity, innovation, risk taking and creativity – I hear these words a lot in schools as traits and behaviours we want for our children but rarely do we advocate for developing these as leadership behaviours when looking at how to transform our workforces. This was echoed in a recent podcast where I interviewed Richard Gerver who said that, upon leaving headship to have a change in direction within education, it was this exact enactment and living of the values we wish to instil in our learners which has provided him with a great education 'adventure'. If we do what we have always done we will get what we've always got. If we're happy with the status quo then that's just fine, but if we want to explore new ways of working and provide opportunities for our staff to really hone and explore their talents then a limited amount of job types and working structures is not going to facilitate this. In Taylor Swift's 22 she captures the excitement and possibility of standing on the cusp of the rest of your adult life with all its uncertainty but also opportunity. If we are to remain as upbeat as Taylor Swift's 22 and keep our system evolving and fresh then we must not grow old in our thinking and, as another famous Taylor Swift song says, we must instead take any potentially outdated attitude and fixed mindset and 'Shake It Off'.

Questions to consider

Employers	Flexible workers
Is there an opportunity to create new roles alongside or instead of traditional roles? Why might we want them? What do we want to do which current roles might preclude us from doing? Could a newly created role create the space and flex for us to innovate and be creative?	How will you establish presence in your new role? How will you establish yourself within a team as a flexi worker? Can you utilise social media or networking to develop links?
Are we aware of who are our lone workers in our organisations? What check in and support mechanisms do we have in place for them?	Do you have regular scheduled catch ups to review projects, wellbeing and workload?
For those who are part-time or lone workers, how do we embed their presence within our wider workforce? How do we ensure they are not disenfranchised, forgotten or sidelined?	How much freedom do you have to drive and innovate with your work? How much do you rely on direction and how much is self directed?
How much direction do we give our staff? Is there enough 'hands off' approach to kindle creative thinking?	If yours is a newly created role have you absolute clarity around your job description and expectations?

Track twelve: All These Things That I've Done

The Killers

If you've ever seen a slightly lacklustre attendance on a dancefloor at a party and then watched as someone has put on something by The Killers then you can guarantee that floor will be full and bouncing before you can say 'Mr Brightside'. It appears that Mr Brightside is the universal call for anyone who has a voice in their chest and bounce in their feet. In fact, for a while, I set it as my ringtone for when my brother called me as I had such fond memories of dancing along to it with all my nearest and dearest at his wedding. However, I didn't end up having much luck with that ringtone, instead it served as the soundtrack to one of the most stressful moments of my career.

During our initial Ofsted feedback meeting with our chair of governors, lead inspector, local authority representative and Claire, my phone started screaming the lyrics from Mr Brightside as my brother called my phone. I frantically searched for the damn thing to turn it off but I couldn't find it anywhere as Claire and I had tidied up a bit. I'd ended up leaving it on top of the filing cabinet which then got some paper stacked on it. And so, as Brandon Flowers yelled his lyrics at the entire room, I was sweating, panicking and desperately trying to locate the thing to shut it up. I eventually found it, panicked again and simply opened the office door and lobbed the phone Basil Fawlty style then sat down smiling at a rather bemused inspector (and Claire stifling a laugh) and picked up my pen as if nothing had happened. It was typical that he was only ringing to see how we had got on that day and check I was OK.

It was also a Killers song 'All These Things That I've Done' that I used to make a photo montage for a colleague's leaving assembly. The slideshow detailed all the things that our colleague had achieved that had made a huge difference to all aspects of school life and had a positive effect on so many staff, pupils and their families. I love a good leaving assembly but I always think it a little sad that we leave it until someone is leaving to truly, fully and publicly celebrate all the things they have done. It is the collation and curation of all the things that we do in our careers which can be the key to the next milestone development in our collective thinking about flex. One thing I have learnt about flexible working is that not only does it provide balance, creativity, innovation and reform for organisations but it allows the flexible worker to have a much less linear approach to their career development.

I spoke recently at an online flex event organised by Hannah Wilson about not having a blanket approach to flexible working and discussed the benefits of 'patchwork' flex. There is a temptation to try and systemise the way we integrate flexible working into our organisations and to adopt a new narrative of 'this is how we do flex here', which ironically is more rigid than it is flexible (I'll discuss 'rigid flexibility' later in the book). When we think of flexible working and we look at the Department for Education for definitions of it, nowhere does it talk about combination or patchwork flexibility. During Hannah's event, I showed a handmade patchwork blanket that I'd had made for my third baby when he was born. Instead of it being a big block of a single colour or a set of disparate smaller pieces, it was a beautiful blend of complementary sections, colours and patterns which were all bound and sewn together. When we think about flexible working patterns we need to push the flex narrative even more and not think about it simply as one job with home commitments but explore the potential of patchwork flexibility. By this I mean capitalising on the potential which flex provides to explore multiple possible working patterns. Nowhere is it written that there should be a single job for the flexible worker and this is potentially where the flex model reaps its greatest rewards for both employer and flexible worker.

A flexible worker may want the security which a part-time role provides but which also then provides scope to undertake additional work or study. This multi-flex approach means that the flexible worker is truly in control of their working patterns and can pursue additional areas of interest or complementary roles. There is somewhat of a situation of 'missing a trick' for many when thinking about multi-flex as what it provides is not only a broader and more diverse skillset and experience but also the potential to use and apply this expertise and knowledge in multiple settings, thus enhancing the work in all of the multi-flexers workplaces. This is especially true if the work the multi-flexer takes part in broadens networks or is in an area of particular specialism. It is not unlike undertaking additional training and development which then benefits all involved, including the multi-flexer themselves as they have a broader professional network to call upon, multiple experiences to inform their view of the sector, additional shared knowledge and expertise from colleagues in different roles and all the time whilst getting paid for this broadening of experience. It also allows for the multi-flexer to organise their flexible working practices in different ways. They may be undertaking one body of work where they are contracted to be in a school on certain days but they may also be working in a different additional multi-flex roles to develop educational materials, speak at events, support or coach online, write, volunteer, study or complete the same or similar work in a contrasting setting.

This multi-flex approach means that some or all of the work can be carried out at different times which has the potential to allow the multi-flexer to not be tied to traditional working hours or to a school setting full time. It also allows for additional study and it is interesting to note that some postgraduate courses in education require students to be working in school for a set number of days per week. This in itself needs a shake-up as it is flexible workers who potentially have the greatest amount of flex in their weeks to fit in and complete the associated study. Precluding a colleague from taking a course because they work part-time is another example of the ingrained 'full time is best' narrative and bias and one which, if not addressed is another developmental door slammed in the faces of our flexible workers. A multi-flex patchwork approach means that we develop highly skilled, multi-experienced colleagues who can apply their knowledge and skills in different roles simultaneously across the sector.

Employers should be aware of the real benefits that encouraging multi-flex employees to be part of their workforces can bring. Just like the patchwork blanket I shared on the flex event, it is possible to create and curate professional experiences to build a diverse but complementary set of knowledge skills and experiences that create a unique and bespoke career 'patchwork blanket'. Discussions around career development, performance management, coaching, career opportunities and the development of new roles in our organisations should recognise and include the benefits of developing, employing and championing multi-flexing as a real and genuine positive career choice. Just like this chapter's track from The Killers, the aim would be to not pigeonhole everyone with the somewhat limited historical range of career routes but to champion multi-flexing so those who choose to embrace multi-flexing can proudly lay out their patchwork blankets as 'All These Things That I've Done'.

Questions to consider

Employers	Flexible workers
How much of your appraisal or staff performance reviews focus on individual career aspirations and opportunity? How much is focused on getting to know staff's individual circumstances and how working patterns and CPD opportunities might be best structured to develop and nurture this?	How could multi-flex or patchwork flex benefit your work/life balance, study and/or ongoing development?
Are there any multi-flexers currently in your organisation? Who are they and what do they do? At which level do they work and in which roles? How does their multi-flexing affect the impact of their work within your organisation? Are there bodies of work or projects which could be offered as multi-flex opportunities?	Are there multiple part-time commitments you would be interesting in combining? How might these slot together?
Is there a 'blanket' approach to flexible working in your organisation? How often are working patterns and structures evaluated for effectiveness including retention, opportunity for career development, contract type and narrative around availability?	Have you considered discussing multi-flex with your family and your employers? What would be the benefits and challenges for both groups?
Are projects or bodies of work advertised as being open to flexible workers as well as full roles? Are these advertised outside the organisation as well as within to attract a wider pool of talent and expertise?	How much is your total available 'work' time budget if it is not constrained by school hours (e.g. including evenings or weekends) how many hours would you realistically want to devote to work or study? How many hours or sections of time could you or would you be willing to devote to each role?
How many of your current flexible workers work in the same or similar ways? Are their views about the efficacy of these setups discussed in performance reviews and/or career coaching?	Have you left enough space in your time budget for yourself? Have you overfilled the time budget so that it is full to the brim with work and home commitments or is there some 'wriggle room' for leisure and wellbeing?

Employers	Flexible workers
How many employees are undertaking additional study, volunteering or speaking/ writing commitments outside their current roles? How does this contribute to the pool of talent within the staff? How can additional opportunities be flagged up?	How much do you need to earn in order to meet your financial commitments? How much of your total earnings would each role pay? Have you considered how you might tackle a tax self assessment or managing your own finances if part of your earnings now mean some of your income is in addition to and outside your usual role or job with your employer?
How can boards or trusts use examples of freelance or multi-flex working models from outside education to help shape opportunity within the education organisation?	Have you got clearly defined career and life goals? Have you considered coaching to help establish these? Are you aware of what makes you happy and what you are trying to achieve in terms of fulfilment?
	What are you really good at or really interested in? Is there potential to pursue elements of this within multi-flex? How might you go about this?

Track thirteen: Solid

Ashford and Simpson

There's a phrase I coined a little while ago when asked to speak about flexible working and it's 'rigid flexibility'. The Ashford and Simpson song 'Solid' is about a relationship where things go a bit wrong but they've now recovered. It can be a little like this when setting up flexible working. We've already talked about 'blanket flexibility' where employers, the wider sector and employees think of flexible working in only one way rather than exploring the multiple nuances, structures and models it can include. Rigid flexibility is where either employer or employee is so fixed in their view or expectation of the flexible working arrangement that it becomes unwieldy, unworkable or simply not viable.

When I talk about rigid flexibility it's usually accompanied with a slide containing a picture of a tug of war between two people who are holding a coiled phone flex. This is because there should *not* be a tug of war between the employee and employer, instead they should be putting communication (hence the phone cord) at the heart of any planning or decision making around flexible working. We have already covered how, when applying for a flexible working arrangement, there needs to be a realistic stance from both the employer and employee and an understanding that it is a right to request, not a right to be either immediately granted or dismissed. Each flexible working request needs to be considered as an individual case which is why 'rigid flexibility' should be avoided. There needs to be a realistic, honest and open discussion about what the needs of the organisation are and what the possible options for the employee are. Each request will be sitting against a backdrop of multiple other factors, both at home and in the organisation, and no one should underestimate just how emotionally loaded these requests can be. The juggling of finances, caring, adjusting to new work and life patterns are all happening for the employee and then the juggling of timetables, staffing, communication and training are in the mind of the employer. However this should not be a meeting in which the one with the greatest poker face emerges victorious, it should be an open discussion about the possible models of flexible working, the expectations of employer and employee, and should feel as supportive as possible for all involved.

Once in that role though there is another aspect of rigid flexibility. As a part-time teacher and leader, I had days for which I was paid and days for which I was not. Sometimes, at the last minute, these needed moving, such as during an inspection or when a specific training event I needed to attend was being held on a non-working day. In addition to these last-minute 'big' things, there were often smaller things which a colleague would need to talk to me about. Now it would be really easy to be absolutely rigid about my working hours and days and say 'I don't work on these days so I am 100% uncontactable'. However, this is not necessarily practical or helpful in the long run. If Claire needed to know where I had put the key to the filing cabinet or which file I had put a particular report in then a quick phone call would save her hours and simply be the sensible thing to do and I would do the same with her. What we didn't do was phone each other up with long-winded discussions that required concentration or significant input, those were left for designated work time. In addition to this, we had an unspoken agreement that for really big things – such as Ofsted or a local authority meeting, big whole school events and full governors' meetings – we would both be there, regardless of the day of the week. Sometimes we'd take this back in lieu but other times we just recognised that it was a one-off part of the role. We would never have dreamt of leaving the other one to carry out a major piece of work or event without the other one there.

In fact, the school had another Ofsted inspection not long after I left and I remember driving to school the day I had heard about it to ask if there was anything I could do and I didn't even work there anymore! This is not because I am some kind of martyr but because I never worked flexibility with 'rigid flexibility'. Flexible working is not a one-way stretch. It is a two-way relationship where the flex is both ways. This doesn't mean that the flexible worker should not be paid properly, expected to work on days when they are not contracted without negotiation or made to feel as if they are not pulling their weight, but equally there needs to be a recognition that on occasions it is easier overall to take a quick phone call or attend an additional session rather than insisting on rigid structures in a flexi setup. This is not about not protecting or not ringfencing the employee's time or wellbeing but is more often about common sense. The best and most successful flexible working setups I have seen over the last 14 years are the ones which are truly flexible rather than rigidly flexible. This builds true partnership and understanding of both the needs of the employer and the employee. It is about developing the kind of relationship and professional respect to understand the needs of both parties and to use the flex model to best effect, both in terms of setting up the arrangement but not then being too 'solid' and forming a rigidly flexible structure.

Questions to consider

Employers	Flexible workers
Do we regularly evaluate our communication systems to ensure that colleagues know when they are expected to check, respond to or can leave until their working days our emails, messages, etc? Have we considered any part-time workers when we are dealing with or communicating deadlines? Are they being expected to deal with things in a much shorter timeframe or shoulder more work pro rata than their full-time colleagues?	How can I ensure that I can respond to one-offs and/or emergencies without impacting on my non-working days? Have I clearly communicated my availability including any additional times when I may have some flex in order to attend events or respond to queries which would be convenient. Have I communicated times or days on which I am definitely not available for additional work?
Do we encourage digital courtesy across our organisations in terms of communication and do we ensure that our processes are regularly reviewed as new technology and communication software is integrated?	Do I keep accurate records of additional work I have undertaken over and above my usual role and do I ensure I keep lines of communication open and clear by asking before agreeing to additional work that any additional work is paid, time in lieu or part of my directed time? Do I regularly check in with my line managers to review my workload and working hours?
Have we established with part-time or flexi colleagues which events, instances or circumstances might necessitate additional hours? Have we clearly communicated in good time information about lieu, additional payments or increases in contracted hours for these? Are key dates for additional hours given out in advance and kept to a minimum?	If I am job-sharing, have we got clear shared and understood boundaries and guidelines about how we will communicate on any non-working days?
Are flexible workers' diaries and commitments regularly reviewed in order to ensure they are in receipt of appropriate additional payment or lieu? How often are they reviewed and by whom? Do our flexible workers have adequate lines of communication for discussing their workload and commitments?	

Track fourteen: Stand By Me

Ben E. King

This song came about as a favourite after falling in love with pretty much all of the cast of *Stand By Me* when I was younger, especially River Phoenix. I still can't watch this film without feeling 12 years old again and remembering how I'd stare dreamily at the screen, entranced by one of the best coming-of-age films. It's also one of the most successful songs of all time with over 400 different recordings. I'm yet to meet anyone who hears it and doesn't start singing or nodding along. I played it in the waiting room of a teams training call I was hosting the other day with my camera off and it was amazing to see dozens of colleagues joining the meeting and swaying and singing along before we started. It's instantly recognisable from the first few notes and is truly an absolute classic.

I love the sentiment of standing by someone regardless of what catastrophe or apocalyptic scene could unfold. It takes courage to truly stand by something you believe in, go against the grain and do something innovative, creative or different. Our educational organisational systems are due a coming-of-age blockbuster moment when it comes to flexible working. There are thousands of flexi workers out there working in multiple different setups but we are yet to convince all voices that this is a good thing. The belief that 'full-time is best' is still the pervasive narrative in education and there needs to be a lot of united work if we are to turn this ship around. The objection to the sharing of a role especially is one that is seemingly rather unique to education too. No one questions a shift change of nursing or medical staff in a hospital; it is accepted that here trained professionals are trusted to communicate key information and maintain continuity of care, often in life-threatening situations. No one bats an eyelid when, in pre-school and nursery, children have multiple key workers. Yet, there is this fixed mindset for some that one teacher for one group, class or set of students is preferable.

The fact that teaching hours and 'directed time' are also directed so rigidly as to be farcical is another aspect we need to address. I spoke recently to a teacher who told me their head checks that all staff (every teacher and staff member at every level) are on-site from 8:30am to 4:30pm every day and actively challenges anyone who arrives after or leaves earlier than these times; they even go as far as to check the 'clocking in and out' via the tracking of the use of the staff's electronic fobs which open the school doors. This is a complete but sadly not all too rare example of the infantilisation of our profession and is definitely not treating colleagues as the highly-qualified, academic professionals they are. I would also be asking myself what other tasks headteachers have chosen to not do by focusing their leadership energies on monitoring their entire staff's daily movements in and out of the building.

When we think about our profession, we have almost all successfully completed tertiary education including a postgraduate qualification. This same highly-qualified and trusted profession, who have managed their own significant academic study, juggled placements, rigorous assessments, who can manage a group of 30 young people, plan, assess, demonstrate excellent people skills, motivate and inspire a generation is then treated by some as if they cannot be trusted to get a bit of work done at home or to manage their own diaries. It is madness. Yes, you can verify someone's identity for their passport as a fine upstanding trusted professional but woe betide if you decide you want to sort out your own working pattern and complete your data analysis after the kids have gone to bed or you've done your reading for your master's degree in Costa for a couple of hours at the end of the school day. One aspect of lockdown was that some of the micro-management of people's time and an insistence that we are all on-site for specific times of the day and clearly visible had to dissipate.

As I mentioned previously, what lockdown proved was that colleagues would and could still complete work without having to be present in school all of the time. They demonstrated that not only are they highly qualified but hugely adaptable and would still get everything done without the need to be in a draughty classroom or sitting around a table in front a pile of rather sad biscuits and a collection of mismatched 'greatest teacher' mugs containing pretty poor quality coffee. Lockdown has worked in flexible working's favour as it has provided a real-time lived example of just how much of the school day and its associated tasks can be flexed. Yes, the ideal going forward will probably be a blend of face-to-face and flexed working as I'm fairly sure we all fell out of love with total online communication despite the ability to conduct a leadership meeting in your PJ bottoms and your slippers. I know I developed digital fatigue and 'Zoom neck' pretty quickly and I desperately missed my colleagues and the very human aspects of learning and development which are facilitated by being a collective in the same room – not least the fact that you can't use my beloved huge sugar paper and felt tips online. But what it did show was that even with people being forced to not leave their houses unless absolutely necessary, the world carried on, the sun came up every morning and work was still turned in on time. Not only that but work was turned in on time in the middle of a global pandemic when often juggled alongside the potential second full-time job of home-schooling or caring for friends and family, the uncertainty of the global situation and an undercurrent of fear and the unknown. Now if teachers can turn in work on time and adapt with speed, agility, dedication and adaptability surely they can have their PPA off-site, leave early to pick up their own children or be trusted to complete work at home when they're not also juggling lockdown demands?

I would never advocate that colleagues should not meet face-to-face and dash off-site at any opportunity, as we've already outlined there is the need to have those incidental communications, to build relationships and to develop a feeling of community and shared purpose. What I would also not advocate is a blanket approach to all colleagues having to always be in during certain hours of every day unless they have a direct teaching responsibility. Not only is completing work at home often more efficient as there are fewer distractions but it also cuts out commuting time which means there is a larger time budget for the working day. When completing a specific piece of work such as a detailed data analysis or the production of a complicated document, Claire or I would often complete this at home to have clear thinking time and absolute focus. All too often working from home in education is equated with some fictional scene of a lie-in, feet up in front of daytime TV and a cursory flicking open of the laptop. The sheer work rates teachers demonstrated during lockdown has hopefully smashed this myth and proven that working from home for specific projects and pieces of work is both beneficial and efficient.

Some may argue that teachers 'get enough holidays already' to not have to want or need flexible working practices. What school holidays mean in reality though is many teachers using the first few days or weeks to recover physically and mentally from an unsustainable work rate which was maintained during term time but can carry on no longer. Add in then the life admin type appointments which need sorting such as dentist and doctor visits, car MOTs, health checks, house repairs and so on, and you begin to see that the very inflexible nature of the school term working patterns actually mean that educators have to cram a disproportionate amount of 'life' into the school holidays rather than luxuriating on a sun lounger for six weeks. The fact that there are so few exceptions for teachers to take time off as well is another much-overlooked fact. I have heard countless times of staff denied opportunities to attend funerals, children's graduations, nativity plays or solicitor's appointments. This is again an infantilisation and a refusal to accept that teachers are humans with real lives. Unlike other professions where periods of leave can be requested during the majority of the year, teachers are not afforded the same opportunities and so every time a little bit of life happens they either have to accept that they cannot be involved in it or they have to actively schedule it for the school holidays. It is no surprise that few teachers get married in April, May or June but there are always a flurry of August weddings!

This is not meant to sound like a misery competition where teaching is pitted against other jobs but it is another aspect of the role which needs to be factored in when talking about flex. If the wider world of work contains 42% of women working flexibly but only 26% in education then there is a lot of catching up to do both in terms of contractual changes, expectations from leaders and the structure of our working practices. When I came to write this chapter last night I chanced upon a thread on Twitter retweeted hundreds of times which was about part-time working in education; it had been written in response to another thread which was a criticism of shared teaching roles. There was overwhelming support from people who had worked successfully in part-time or shared roles for many years and they shared their success stories to highlight the issue. Initially I was delighted that this was being discussed but then was soon disappointed when I realised that it was necessary because there was still this pervasive 'full-time is best' narrative. It should not be up to the flexi workers out there to have to justify the success or otherwise of their individual setups. Each one of those professionals will have gone through a process whereby their working patterns will have been negotiated by multiple senior leaders and once granted that should be that. If we are mistrusting the effectiveness of part-time or flexi workers then what we are also doing is mistrusting the judgement of those who have been entrusted with employing them.

On reading the thread there, despite hundreds of retweets and comments, and thousands of likes, there was something still absent – the voices of those who employ, lead and support our flexible workers. What was missing were the leadership allies; those professionals who are innovative and creative enough to recognise the potential benefits and the real opportunities for their organisations which flexi workers can provide. It was as if the flexi workers were standing alone having to justify their position when in actual fact they will have been interviewed, appointed, performance managed and judged to be performing really rather well, thank you very much, by the leaders within our profession but those allies were absent from the discussion.

If we are truly to champion flexible working and see its potential for our sector then the voices we need to hear alongside the case studies of effective individual worked examples are those leaders who are the voices of change and flexi champions. We need not just a thousand individual case studies to create a powerful argument but also the voices of those who employ thousands. We need the decision-makers to stand up and say 'I believe in this'. We need them to become flex-perts and to advocate for flexible workers at every opportunity. This is one of the main reasons I asked Sam and Jonny to write the foreword to this book. Between them they are true allies for flexible workers and they are also expert leaders who work full-time in large MATs and all-through schools. Although they are not flexible workers, they can see the benefits of flexible working. We need more Jonnys and Sams in our educational leadership positions to ensure that their innovative, creative and 'human first' approach to staff development is at the heart of what we do across the sector.

We also need those who are potentially not in the position to make the final decision – 'press the red button', so to speak – to be the advocates and allies through the questions they ask. A leader at one level may not be in charge of making the initial or final hiring decisions but they can be the one to ask if the role could be advertised flexibly if there's a possibility we don't need to just replace the old role with exactly the same thing, or if there is someone already in the organisation who might relish taking on part of the role as a job-share. Once the conversations and questions begin then the whole flexi discussion is opened up. Until flexible workers get true allies at all levels across the sector then, sadly, it will be up to the individual to try and justify their role and their impact just like that Twitter thread. In short, what the sector needs are voices to proactively advocate for flexible working, not the flexible workers to have to request, like Ben E. King for someone to 'Stand By Me'.

Questions to consider

Employers	Flexible workers
How do I ensure I communicate professional trust across my organisation? How closely are colleagues' diaries managed – how does this contribute to the development of professional trust and how do I promote a sense of agency and autonomy across my organisation?	Who in my organisation might be a flexible working ally? How might I become a flexible working ally? How can I promote best practice in flexible working, positive attitudes and flex as an aspirational model in my role?
How can I demonstrate allyship regarding flexible working and how can I ensure all stakeholders are also flexible working allies?	How could I encourage more conversations around flexible working in my organisation? Have I signposted groups and organisations who might be of use to other flexible workers?
How does my organisation demonstrate, promote, advertise and promote its approaches to flexible working both within the organisation and across wider networks and communities? How do we develop our organisation's reputation in being flexible friendly?	How can I support/mentor other colleagues who may want to work flexibly? How can I share my flexi knowledge?
Do we actively challenge resistance to flexible working? Do we actively look for innovative solutions such as within the wider world of work or other education organisations? How proactive are we in evolving our understanding of how flexible working could be developed within our organisations? Who do we consult within our discussions around innovation?	How can I utilise new technology to support flexible working, e.g. video conferences and remote learning?

Employers	Flexible workers
Are staff encouraged or permitted to work from home? What are the barriers to this? What affect might it have on staff if working from home or staggered starts on certain days were established?	
What lockdown working practices were positive changes we could continue to use? What were any barriers and how might we overcome these?	
What might be the impact on wellbeing, retention and recruitment if we were flexible working advocates and allies? Who might be averse to changing practice? Are we prioritising absolute fairness for all staff over common sense?	
How do we celebrate our successes in promoting flexible working? Have we looked to have our approaches shared more widely in educational publications, e.g. 'Impact', the journal of the Chartered College of teaching, or accredited by organisations such as the GEC?	

Track fifteen: We're All In This Together
The Cast of High School Musical

My children are currently obsessed with *High School Musical*. As a result, the soundtrack is on loop, there is a basketball hoop outside my kitchen, and I am close to tearing my own ears off. However, I will admit to secretly loving bits of it. Don't get my wrong, Sharpay's behaviour at that country club in *High School Musical 2* (oh yes, they love the whole ruddy trilogy) leaves a lot to be desired but I do love the whole 'in it together' mentality and the highlighting of decision making to always do the right thing (see Troy on the horns of a dilemma singing 'Scream' in *High School Musical 3* – see I told you I've watched it many, many times; I think it could actually be my Mastermind subject thanks to my kids' obsession). Despite it being more saccharine than a litre of diet cola, I do kinda like it, just not that much that I'd have chosen to watch it for (at one point) 47 consecutive lockdown days – thanks, kids.

The idea that we're all in this together is not just the preserve of the East High cheerleaders, musicians, actors and basketball stars of *High School Musical* but it should be one of the combining factors of our profession. As educators most of us will have entered the profession because we wanted to make a difference, to encourage young people and to provide the best educational experience we could for them. Few of us in our profession will wake up in the morning and decide that the order of the day is to deliberately do a shocking job and make a complete fudge of whatever we do. With this in mind, we genuinely are all in this together. Whatever part of the sector is our specialism, our current role or the one we aspire to have, we are all in the same game. We're all playing for the same trophy or accolade and that is not one for ourselves, it is the effective education of our young people which is our prize and our uniting team focus. When we start to see ourselves as genuinely all in this together then we begin to recognise that we can't all do the same job in the same way.

When we look around at our colleagues in our immediate workplaces and across our wider networks we see people at different stages of their lives. We see new parents, colleagues with long-term or temporary health challenges, colleagues amid relationship breakdowns or bereavements, we see colleagues who are juggling caring for relatives, extended commutes, financial pressures, pension worries, housing issues, living with abuse or violence, colleagues who want to do further study, colleagues who are also working to support a partner or family's business, colleagues who want further experience in other settings, colleagues who are keen to progress their careers and others who need a permanent or temporary step aside or down, we see experienced colleagues, colleagues close to retirement, new entrants to the profession, career changers the list is endless. With hundreds and thousands of teachers and educators across our nation, it surely can't be that we expect them all to work full-time and in the historical ways in which we have always worked. We need the innovative thinking for models such as pairing the aspirant head with the existing head who wants to semi-retire and doing a co-headship for several years; we need part-time training routes into teaching so we establish teaching as a family and life-friendly profession from the word go, not peddling putting your life on hold for two years because your training and NQT years mean you'll barely have time to sleep, breathe or nip for a wee let alone have a life.

We need flexible working models to be proactively suggested and advertised not just 'requested'. A request implies that you are asking for something unusual (remember 'Please sir, can I have some less?') and with 42% of women in the wider world of work already working flexibly then it's definitely not unusual in the world beyond the school gates. Being in it together also means becoming more representative in terms of our flexible workforce too. With only 8% of men working flexibly in education then the discussion around opportunities for men to work flexibly alongside their female flex contemporaries is an area for further exploration. It is interesting to note that women in education remain underrepresented in leadership positions and it is of further interest still when this is correlated with the marked difference between the number of men and women who are working flexibly in education. More flexi leadership roles are beginning to develop but a more balanced picture of flex across men and women across the profession is also an area for focus. Flexible working offers so many opportunities for further study, enhanced experience in multiple settings and career progression that it is a hugely underused model across our sector. But these are changes which cannot be made effectively or at pace with single voices. We need for employers, employees, trusts, boards and organisations to realise that we are ultimately working towards the same goal of great outcomes for our pupils. We cannot be providing that to best effect if we are haemorrhaging talent each year and heading into a huge both recruitment and retention crisis. We cannot provide excellence for our pupils if we do not first recognise the excellence in our profession and hang onto it for dear life.

One final point about flex which I have deliberately left until this final track is that it is not necessarily forever. A flexible working request, if granted, is not the Magna Carta. It does not have to endure forevermore in one single incarnation. When we agree to flex, that's what it is, flexible. I have worked flexibly during co-headship, as a class teacher, a senior leader and now in my current trust role. I have chopped, changed, flexed and fiddled around with my days to meet both mine and the needs of whichever organisation I am working for. Flexible working and granting of a flexible working request is not the beginning of the end or 'setting a precedent which everyone will end up wanting', it is being responsive to the changing needs of the workforce and preserving talent and experience within our profession. People's lives change constantly and so also, therefore, is the ever-changing potential of the flex model. If you have all full-time staff, you have zero flex to respond to any changes you may want to make or need. With a blend of full-time and flex or 100% flex, you have inbuilt flex with which you can respond to the needs of the pupils and the school, plus you get happy colleagues with manageable workloads who potentially also have space in their lives for further study or professional experiences. So we can either continue as we are or we can begin to *really* talk about flex. We can talk about it at every level in our organisation and we can begin to dismantle some of the beliefs, systems and practices which mean that so many of our trained and talented workforce have already left or are leaving. So maybe you know how you'll start grabbing your East High edu-pom poms and becoming a flexi cheerleader, or maybe you need to think a little more about the potential and the impact flex could have on you, your life or your organisation. However you're feeling, I hope you begin to look at flex a little differently and – like Troy in *High School Musical 3* when he successfully manages to combine basketball and performing (sorry – spoiler) – end up able to combine all of your passions because, however you want to look at the education recruitment and retention crisis, 'We're All In This Together'.

The after party

Many of the people who have been kind enough to read this book and review it for me have suggested that I set up a Spotify playlist for the book. I'm guessing one will appear but in addition to the book playlist, which doesn't necessarily reflect my musical taste, I thought I'd share with you the playlist I usually whack on when on my way to an event to speak or which I have on in my actual house for my kitchen discos.

These events are so important to me, they are where I discovered whole communities of educationalists who are passionate advocates of flexible working and who are working tirelessly within our system to ensure that there is creativity, aspiration, innovation and equity for all of our flexi workers and flexi organisations. Those events were the catalyst for this book so events such as BrewEds and WomenEd events, those organised by the GEC and by individuals such as Kat Howard have meant that I've met so many people who are just as dedicated to developing a generation of flex-perts as I am. And, just like an after party at an event or in the kitchen at a house party, you'll find this is where the real fun and creativity is occurring.

Meeting people like Sam and Jonny at Kat's book launch; meeting Sam Twiselton, Dame Alison Peacock, Adrian Bethune and Dr Emma Kell at BrewEds; the WomenEd community at national and regional events, and then the magic of Twitter where I've connected with people like Nic Ponsford who is doing amazing work with the GEC and organisations as Flexible Teacher Talent, the Shared Headship Network and @ MaternityCPD have shown me that I'm not alone in this field. And that is what I want to leave you with, the message that you are not alone. Whether you're an individual wanting to know more about flexibility, an organisation wanting to shake up the way you flex in your own workplaces or you're someone determined to take on rigid or outdated systems in your own organisations, then I want to let you know you are not on your own. There is so much happening on the flexi dancefloor right now so pull on your dancing shoes, turn up the volume and whack on an edu floor-filler. As Jonny says in his part of the foreword, I hope you dance.

Happy adventuring,

Em.

The flexi playlist

Heroes (We Could Be) – Alesso

Brave – Sara Bareilles

Make Your Own Kind of Music – Paloma Faith

Fighter – Christina Aguilera

Almost There – Anika Noni Rose

Breakin' Down The Walls of Heartache – Johnny Johnson & The Bandwagon

Salute – Little Mix

Dancing – Kylie

You Can Get It If You Really Want It – Desmond Deckker

Great Things – Echobelly

Here Comes the Sun – The Beatles

It Ain't What You Do – The Fun Boy Three and Bananarama

Shake It Off – Taylor Swift

Think – Aretha Franklin

This Could Be My Moment – The Verve

We Dance On – N-Dubz ft. Bodyrox

We Are Family – Sister Sledge

Harder Better Faster – Daft Punk

The Only Way Is Up – Yazz & The Plastic Population

Fight Song – Rachel Platten

Rachel Plattern – Fight Song

It Takes Two – Marvin Gaye & Kim Weston

CPSIA information can be obtained
at www.ICGtesting.com
Printed in the USA
JSHW011928070221
11557JS00004B/5